Obituaries in American Culture

Janice Hume

University Press
of Mississippi
Jackson

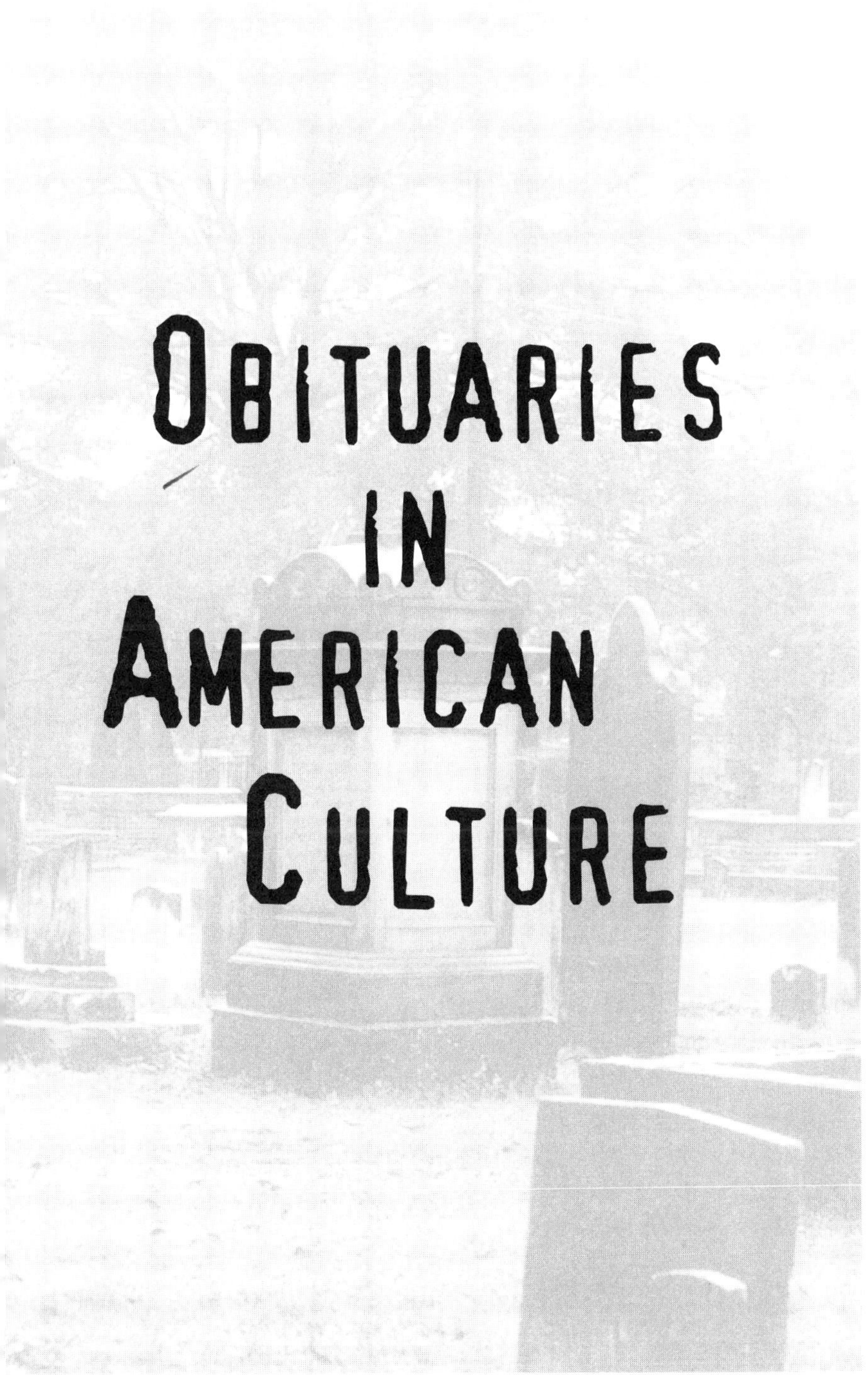

OBITUARIES IN AMERICAN CULTURE

www.upress.state.ms.us

Manufactured in the United States of
America

08 07 06 05 04 03 02 01 00 4 3 2 1
∞

Photographs on pages 2, 3, and 5 courtesy of *The Mobile Register*

Library of Congress Cataloging-in-Publication

Hume, Janice.
Obituaries in American culture / Janice Hume.
p. cm
Includes bibliographical references and index.
ISBN 1-57806-241-1 (cloth : alk. paper) — ISBN 1-57806-242-X (paper : alk. paper)
1. United States—Civilization—19th century. 2. United States—Civilization—20th century. 3. United States—Civilization—Sources. 4. Obituaries—United States—History. 5. Death—Social aspects—United States. 6. Memory—Social aspects—United States. I. Title.

E169.1 .H94 2000
973.5—dc21

99-052868

British Library Cataloging-in-
Publication Data available

Contents

Acknowledgments

Special thanks to Professor Betty Houchin Winfield of the University of Missouri School of Journalism for her invaluable guidance. Thanks also to MU Professors John Merrill, Lee Wilkins, Robert Collins, and Steven Watts and Kansas State University Professor Paul Parsons for their expertise and support.

Thanks also to my family, especially my parents, Marcus F. Hume and Norma Pickens Hume.

Obituaries in American Culture

A RECORD
FOR
PUBLIC MEMORY

When fifty-year-old Virginian William P. Custis died "after a long and wasting illness" in 1838, readers of the *Daily National Intelligencer* learned about his generous hospitality, his sterling business principles, and his kindness as a neighbor and husband. Custis's newspaper obituary not only recorded the "fact" of his death but celebrated the virtues of his life, saying, "In paying a tribute to one who has gone to the dead, it is due to his memory publicly to record his virtues. There is in the life of a noble, independent and honest man, something so worthy of imitation, something that so strongly commends itself to the approbation of a virtuous mind, that his name should not be left in oblivion, nor his influence be lost."[1] Thus, Custis's obituary provided comfort for his grieving friends and family and enlightened others in his community. The obituary expressed publicly a sense of the value of his particular life, the life of one American. Today this published obituary, like many others of the era, offers a fascinating glimpse into some of the cultural idiosyncrasies of Custis's America by highlighting specific attributes of this citizen such as his independence, honesty, and virtuous mind. His newspaper obituary emphasizes particular salient aspects of his life and thus reflects his society's cultural values.

The obituary, or death notice, has long been a regular feature in the American press. For more than two hundred years newspapers have recorded for the public the lives and the virtues of American citizens. An obituary distills the essence of a citizen's life, and because it is a commemoration as well as a life chronicle, it reflects what society values and wants to remember about that person's history. Early-American news providers set the standard for newspaper obituaries;[2] thus, the systematic examination of obituaries can provide a useful tool for exploring the changing values of Americans of any era. Such an examination can help in understanding an important aspect of American culture, the public memory of its citizens.

Obituaries link published memories of individual lives with generational, or family, memory and with American collective memory. They add to the understanding of American journalistic history by showing how news practices associated with the rise of the mass press might historically have influenced death notices. Perhaps most important, they offer insight into American values. For example, specific values emphasized in obituaries changed significantly following major turning points in the nation's political and cultural history, times when the nation was becoming more inclusive. In these eras—Andrew Jackson's presidency, the Civil War and, the years surrounding the granting of women's suffrage—the new inclusion was reflected not only in who was commemorated in newspaper obituaries but also in how they were remembered. Thus, obituaries highlight era ethical issues of virtue and exclusion.

A systematic inspection of obituaries can be a tool for exploring cultural history. Fredric F. Endres found that frontier obituaries reflected cultural values, especially the value of life: almost everyone, regardless of age, sex, or station in life on the American frontier, "deserved some sort of meaning being given to their lives."[3] But a study of obituaries published in Boston and New York newspapers more than one hundred years later found a clear pattern of masculine preference, giving "subtle confirmation of the greater importance of men" in twentieth-century American cities.[4] Obituary exclusion, too, can be an important element of understanding.

Public Worth

Obituaries could contribute to a society's well-being by strengthening it collectively and by highlighting the importance of its individual members. Since an obituary is an idealized account of a citizen's life, a type of commemoration meant for public consumption, obituaries should be studied in light of their relationship with the collective, or public, memory, that "body of beliefs about the past that help a public or society understand both its past and its present, and, by implication, its future."[5] Publication of an obituary in the mass media constitutes a rare instance in a democracy when an individual can become part of collective thought, part of what Americans might believe in common about the worth of a life. Obituaries illustrate how the national memory of American cultural symbols is reflected in, and thus influences, the commemorations of the lives of individual citizens. For example, when references to George Washington or Daniel Boone serve to illustrate characteristics of ordinary citizens generations after the passing of these icons, memories of individuals and collective memory are connected and publicly legitimized. Thus, there is a link, a symbiotic relationship, between published commemorations of individual lives and public memory.

Memory is, of course, necessary for the survival of both individuals and societies, and the needs of both can dictate the substance of what is remembered. Psychologist Alan D. Baddeley has written about the "context-dependency" effect on individual memory, meaning that memory often is dictated by a person's current circumstance. He says that people are more likely to remember information relevant to their situation rather than to some distant setting or situation.[6] Societies, too, have the capacity to "remember" and "forget," and this situational relevance plays a role in determining what citizens believe, collectively, about their history. Those collective social memories are also based on current needs. Indeed, newspaper obituaries not only reveal something about what society remembers but also offer hints into what may have been "forgotten" about the attributes and values associated with individual lives.

A wealth of scholarship exists on American public memory, but none specifically links memories of the lives of individual citizens to collective national thought. Why is an obituary link so important? Barry Schwartz calls for an understanding of two distinct aspects of remembering—chronicling and commemoration. He wrote, "Our memory of the past is preserved mainly by means of chronicling, the direct recording of events and their sequence. However, the events selected for chronicling are not all evaluated in the same way. To some of these events we remain morally indifferent; other events are commemorated, i.e., invested with an extraordinary significance and assigned a qualitatively distinct place in our conception of the past. . . . Commemoration celebrates and safeguards the ideal."[7] An obituary certainly lists basic details about the life and death of a citizen, but it also does more. An obituary distills, publishes, and thus legitimizes something more abstract than mere facts. It also reveals values, highlighted in the attributes of the deceased, and should be examined not just as an indifferent chronicle but as a commemoration, a representation of an ideal, with its own distinct contribution to the understanding of history. Those ideals, part of obituary coverage, become safeguarded by their publication.

As Paul Connerton argues in *How Societies Remember*, images of the past often legitimate a current social order.[8] His point could relate to obituaries as legitimizing a "worth," a socially accepted notion of what is important in a life. "It is an implicit rule," he writes, "that participants in any social order must presuppose a shared memory."[9] Obituaries, then, would add to society's shared memory and collective values as well as reflect an individual citizen's adherence to a social norm. Obituaries would tend to ignore deviant behavior or attributes that were socially unacceptable. Shared knowledge or memory, according to Geoffrey Hartman, is an "important yet often unconscious influence on personal identity,"[10] so collective values might naturally influence what is commemorated of the lives of individuals, those values stressed, those attributes and actions highlighted and recounted. Thus, a newspaper obituary might highlight the uniqueness of an individual, or that uniqueness might be subsumed by the needs and values of the collective society.

Families Remembered

Just like collective memory, obituaries combine past and present, public and private. They legitimize characteristics of individual Americans to a collective audience, thus adding to cultural values and memory. And obituaries link public memory not only with individual memory but also with "generational memory," "the memories which individuals have of their own families' history, as well as more general collective memories about the past."[11] This type of memory ties family history with national history by linking individual citizens with specific historic moments. Obituaries that mention, for example, an individual's participation in a famous battle or the gold rush served as an important public declaration of that family's linkage to an important American past. Public memory not only anchors but influences family memory. According to Maurice Halbwachs, "Just as every family quickly acquires a history, and just as its memory becomes enriched from day to day . . . the family progressively tends to interpret in its own manner the conceptions it borrows from society. Each family ends up with its own logic and traditions, which resemble those of the general society."[12] Similarities in citizen obituaries, especially those regarding national experiences, help reveal how society influences the shared memories of citizens and families, thus linking the three types of memory: individual, generational, and public.

Death Stories

Not only can public memory have an impact on obituaries, but death notices of individuals might also influence the collective. Joseph A. Amato argues that death "causes people to tell stories" that can be "shaped by moral judgment, fashioned for the sake of argument, made buoyant by metaphor, or given meaning by the rituals of culture and the promise of religion."[13] Death stories, because of their powerful connection with cultural and religious rituals, fascinate and resonate in a society. Newspaper obituaries are a recognized forum for telling stories of the deaths of individuals as well as for legitimizing those stories for a mass audience. In fact, obituaries share "death stories" of people who have never met, making individual and generational memories an element of public consciousness through the mass media. This phenomenon is necessary, for as Andreas Huyssen argues in his study of public memory in reunited Germany, "The past is not simply there in memory, but it must be articulated to become memory."[14] An obituary, published in the press, articulates virtues of private citizens for assimilation by a society.

But what about the historical accuracy of an obituary as a reflector of an individual life? If it serves to commemorate rather than chronicle, the obituary might seem an unworthy source for scholarly research. Historians are typically concerned with finding out what actually happened rather than what was published in a less-than-trustworthy newspaper. But David Lowenthal warns scholars of the importance of understanding "the screens through which historical information and ideas are commonly filtered."[15] The obituary is a type of screen, providing facts and values filtered by the media and by families of the deceased. Through its written account, it transforms a citizen's life into a type of record, thus giving historians a peek at some of the cultural filtering screens of another era, especially those in the mass media. As Halbwachs writes, "Since a past fact is instructive and a person who has disappeared is an encouragement or an advertisement, what we call the framework of memory is also a concatenation of ideas and judgments."[16] An obituary, the commemoration of the life of someone who has disappeared, would serve to preserve for posterity some of those ideas and judgments that often are so elusive for historians.

American Icons

Studies of the changing symbols in American public memory help to reveal this symbiotic relationship between the memory of an individual life portrayed in an obituary and the accepted values of the collective. Michael Kammen asks, "When and how did the United States become a land of the past, a culture with a discernable memory (or with a configuration of recognized pasts)?"[17] He traces the dialogue of American public memory from just after the American Revolution through 1990. During the early nineteenth century, the strongest symbols in American public memory were associated with the revolution, a shared national experience that served a political need for national strength and unity.[18] But of course those symbols did not remain constant. Through the course of history, people forget, and society changes. Schwartz has traced what he calls the "democratization of George Washington" in collective memory between 1800 and 1865 and found that early recollections of Washington stressed his remoteness and "flawless virtue," while later memories reflected a hero worthy of a more egalitarian nation, showing Washington as an "imperfect man with whom common people could identify."[19] Americans' memories of Washington served their current values and needs. Later, Davy Crockett competed with Washington as a new cultural symbol that, according to Bodnar, represented a break with "monolithic patriotic symbolism." Crockett "stood for common people rather than leaders and for a frontier or regional rather than a national community. . . . The vernacular rather than the official dimension was more powerful in this particular construction of patriotic symbolism than in earlier ones."[20] Crockett embodied the cultural symbol of the pioneer adventurer and served as the consummate egalitarian hero during the Jacksonian era. Americans, Kammen argues, love hero worship, patriotism, and nostalgia, but these tendencies ebb and flow based on present needs.[21] This ebb and flow of cultural symbols also appears in obituaries, in their changing inclusiveness, which shows how one type of symbol, representative of egalitarianism, replaced elite symbols, which stood for a limited or closed citizenry.

The Media's Role

What of the media's role in the evolution of American public memory? Media scholar Daniel Boorstin, in his classic *The Image: A Guide to Pseudo-Events in America,* blames the burgeoning mass media for creating unrealistic public illusions about America's past and present. He argues that Americans live in a "thicket of unreality" created, in large part, because of the mass media.[22] "Americans live in a world where fantasy is more real than reality. . . . The image has more dignity than the original."[23] Boorstin's study shows the origins of American nostalgia in distorted expectations as much as in conflict and sheds light on the influence of changing news conventions on twentieth-century collective memory. Huyssen, too, argues that the media are the primary influence on the way a culture builds its memory. The media, he writes, are the "hidden veil" through which cultural memory and structures of temporality can be viewed.[24] Newspaper obituaries might play at least a small part in creating that "thicket of unreality" and certainly feel the impact of changing press conventions. For example, with the arrival of the penny press, the first truly mass press in America, many newspapers began focusing more on local news, including the deaths of ordinary citizens. The telegraph encouraged brief rather than interpretive news and affected the structure of some obituaries. It certainly gave editors the ability to report quickly the deaths of residents of far-off cities; thus, "telegraph" columns in the 1850s consistently published short obituaries received by wire. Modern obituary writers deal with economic problems of space and often must nail the virtues of a person's life in one hundred words or less.[25] This news convention also affects coverage of the deaths of citizens, what is publicly remembered about their lives.

A public memory that can be distorted by the mass media might also be consciously manipulated. John R. Gillis argues that such memory is not a fixed thing but merely a representation or subjective construction of reality.[26] And Bodnar writes that public memory is political, involving social organization, structure of power, and the meaning of a society's past and present."[27] He examines the commemorative activities in various immigrant communities to show that "for them the past most relevant for the present and worthy of celebration was one that included the values and institutions of the dominant society."[28] Rather than a nation inching toward egalitarianism, Bodnar paints a picture of early Americans engaged in a long struggle to hold onto their individual ethnic identities despite pressure from national interests.[29] Mainstream newspapers, which must appeal to the masses to survive, tend to publish obituaries that reflect the dominant society's cultural construction. But because each obituary is, by definition, the memory of a singular life, it must offer at least something of the individual citizen. The obituary thus provides a glimpse into the complex relationship between individuals and their society.

Public memory is, indeed, an unpredictable commodity. As Kammen says, "Myths and traditions have their own resilience, not completely controllable."[30] Sociologist Michael Schudson argues that American newspapers "are today the most representative carrier and construer and creator of modern public consciousness."[31] And news stories of all kinds—whether about political crises or the deaths of individual citizens—use symbols to hold readers' interest. W. Lloyd Warner writes in *The Living and the Dead: A Study of the Symbolic Life of Americans* that newspapers include "evocative, non-logical symbols rather than logical, empirical ones," representing the "non-logical symbolic beliefs and folk symbols of people who buy the papers."[32] Newspaper obituaries, which carry to the public consciousness those powerful, symbolic death stories, must have at least a small role in influencing collective thought about the past. Obituaries help strengthen the generational linkage so important for Americans' cultural continuity by reflecting what, in death, was most valued about the lives of individual citizens.

The Culture of Death

Changing social attitudes about death in America have almost certainly influenced obituary content. In fact, as Joachim Whaley argues, mourning rituals and religious beliefs are "some of the most important characteristics of any human society."[33] Publishing newspaper obituaries is one way modern humans deal with death and defend life, the obituary's publication providing a sense of finality while celebrating the deceased's noteworthy attributes, preserving and legitimizing these important characteristics of Americans throughout the nation's history. How have Americans faced their mortality? In *Inventing the American Way of Death*, James J. Farrell looks at death as a cultural event in the United States from 1830 to 1950 by examining institutions associated with death. He argues that in American history, death has itself been "dying" as Americans replaced fear of death with a religion-based promise of life: "The social and intellectual changes which affected ideas and institutions of death spanned almost all sectors of American life. . . . Changes in the churches exerted the greatest influence. As the major American religious denominations increasingly stressed a loving, beneficent God, they eased some anxieties which had earlier emanated from religious teachings."[34] In the mid–nineteenth century, however, death was still a major preoccupation. Michael Wheeler writes about the obsessive interest in death in England's Victorian culture, especially in the era's literature and theology, "The existence of a Victorian cult of death implies a measure of social and intellectual homogeneity."[35] Literary deathbed scenes, mourning customs, elaborate funerals, and sentimental funerary art were common in this culture. Americans' customs were comparable to those in England,[36] though in midcentury America, the Civil War added a new dimension to the public's preoccupation with dying. Louise L. Stevenson writes, "In the 1860s and 1870s it was likely that every family had at least one relative participating in the war and facing the probability of death. No wonder that the popular songs of the period dealt with the contingency of death."[37] One way that some Americans dealt with this contingency was through their religious belief that death was simply a passageway to heaven rather than an eternal separation from loved ones. The notion of salvation made easier the acceptance of death as a peaceful end.[38] Numerous studies of Victorian cemeteries and funerary art provide still more evidence about nineteenth-century Americans' religious and sentimental views about the nature of death.[39] So too, obituaries of the era offered some comfort for surviving family and the public about the nature of death. By doing so, obituaries reveal something of American values concerning death and how those values might have changed.

In the twentieth century, however, Americans used science and modern technology to try to wrest control of death, and Farrell argues that funeral reformers indeed succeeded in restructuring the meaning of death. In modern America, funeral directors take care of "death's bodily gruesomeness" and control to a large degree the manner and length of mourning. "But it is a curious kind of control which avoids a confrontation with death. And it is a curious conception of human nature that neglects, for most practical purposes, the biologically limited nature of human life. . . . The denial of death in American society also cuts people off from our common humanity, keeping them at such a distance from the deaths of others that they cannot grieve or mourn except in the culturally prescribed 'way.'"[40] Twentieth-century obituaries deal with death differently than do those in the nineteenth century, influenced in part by this homogeneity and commercialization of American funeral and mourning practices. This new, more commercial, way of death had an impact, too, on the life chronicle, the press commemoration of what was valued about a singular life.

Citizen Inclusion

These ideas about death, commemoration, and American public memory help in understanding the value of the life of the individual citizen in a democracy, a society that, at least in theory, embraces egalitarianism. According to Kammen, "We arouse and arrange our memories to suit our psychic needs," with national memories more likely to be "activated and strengthened by conflict and the desire for reconciliation."[41] Thus, American national memory serves both personal and political ends.

To better understand the relationship between individual and collective memory, it is important to examine newspaper obituaries during times when national debates involved issues of citizen exclusion and reconciliation. In America, then, the most important eras to analyze are those in which citizens demanded and received the right of inclusion in the political franchise. In a democracy, a basic definition of inclusion would be suffrage, but would that political inclusion be reflected on other social levels? Would more and different kinds of individuals be recognized, their attributes recounted publicly in mainstream newspaper obituaries? Changes in obituaries during the Jacksonian, Civil War, and suffrage eras aid in understanding the link between private lives and public virtues in American history.

Media Frames

Obituaries in the media do more than simply relay facts. Obituaries may help distribute a type of ideology to their mass audiences. Framing theory helps scholars understand how that distribution would work. For example, Todd Gitlin argues that the media "specialize in orchestrating everyday consciousness—by virtue of their pervasiveness, their accessibility, their centralized symbolic capacity . . . the mass media produce fields of definition and association, symbol and rhetoric, through which ideology becomes manifest and concrete."[42] He defines *frames* as "principles of selection, emphasis, and presentation composed of little tacit theories about what exists, what happens, and what matters."[43] Zhongdang Pan and Gerald M. Kosicki explain framing as an approach to news discourse. Building on the theories in

Erving Goffman's *Frame Analysis*, Pan and Kosicki conceive of news discourse as a "sociocognitive process" involving "sources, journalists, and audience members operating in the universe of shared culture on the basis of socially defined roles."[44] Because of this relationship between news framing and shared culture, the presentation of any type of news story, including the obituary, is intrinsically linked to memory, culture, and collective meaning.

Though no one has examined, specifically, the framing of newspaper obituaries, scholars have written about the creation and impact of frames in the mass media.[45] Gitlin's study examines the concept in the context of a political movement, while Laura E. Drake and William A. Donohue evaluate its utility for research in conflict resolution.[46] Pippa Norris's *Women, Media, and Politics* argues that "journalists commonly work with gendered frames to simplify, prioritize, and structure the narrative flow of events when covering men and women in public life."[47] Obituaries, too, reflect certain principles of selection, emphasis, and presentation concerning death and the value of a particular life.

Each of four framing categories typically published in newspaper obituaries—name and occupation of the deceased, cause of death, personal attributes of the deceased, and funeral arrangements—offers insight into the cultural values of the three eras as well as news values and practices. For example, names and occupations of the deceased provide evidence of social inclusion or exclusion. Causes of death do more than merely chronicle: they also offer a glimpse into American attitudes about death, as does published information about funeral arrangements. Personal attributes, even virtues, of the deceased reflect changing ideas about what American society values about its individual citizens' lives. Each attribute listed, for example, particularly if the same words or catchphrases are used repeatedly, might indicate a type of promotion of social ideology through framing. The same can be said for names and occupations of the deceased, cause of death, and funeral arrangements, which indicate obituary trends and exceptions to those trends in each era.

Chapter 2 examines 658 obituaries published in two major news publications of the national period, the *Daily National Intelligencer* and *Niles' Weekly Register,* in 1818 and 1838, ten years before and after Andrew Jackson's election to the presidency. The nation was becoming more egalitarian in this era, and more white men received voting rights.

Chapter 3 looks at characteristics of Americans in 3,670 obituaries published in major regional newspapers in sample years before and after the Civil War, a time when Americans were grappling with regional strife, notions of equality, and the inclusion of African American men into the political franchise. This chapter includes obituaries published in the first week of each month of 1855 and 1870 in the *New York Daily Times*, the *New Orleans Picayune*, and the *Baltimore Sun*, again looking at framing devices and categories as windows to understanding how mid-nineteenth-century Americans valued life and dealt with death.

Chapter 4 examines nationally prominent newspapers in sample years before and after the 1920 passage of the Nineteenth Amendment, which gave women the right to vote. As political America became more inclusive, economic and cultural America had moved solidly into an era of consumption, and published obituaries reflect these movements. This chapter includes 4,163 obituaries published in the first week of each month of 1910 and 1930 in the *New York Times*, the *Chicago Tribune*, and, in the West, where the suffrage movement was strongest, the *San Francisco Chronicle*.

Chapter 5 focuses on obituary exclusion. Newspapers do not publish obituaries for every person who dies or list every attribute of even those lives commemorated. Many Americans, in fact, have been excluded, their lives not publicly commemorated. And these exclusions, these textual silences on obituary pages, also reveal something about American values and culture, helping to provide an understanding of exactly who and what were forgotten.

Chapter 6 paints a picture of the changing ideal American as portrayed in obituaries published in prominent general newspapers geared toward the middle and upper classes. For scholars seeking to understand something of the dominant culture's values, these obituaries offer a tiny window to view the worth of the individual citizen's life as placed in public memory. And some 158 years after that "long and wasting illness" took the life of William Custis, his name and virtues—recorded for posterity in his newspaper obituary—can still influence Americans by helping them better understand their culture's history.

THE EGALITARIAN LIFE

Died

In Onondaga, New-York, on the 3d instant, General ASA DANFORTH, aged 72. He was one of our revolutionary patriots, who drew his sword in defense of liberty when success was doubtful and sufferings certain; when his reward was distant, and the pledge insecure; when fame or infamy, independence or slavery, life or death depended on the contingencies of a day. The glorious result left General Danforth an honorable commission, and his country has not been altogether ungrateful for his services. He has filled several stations of trust and honor, with integrity and usefulness, with ability and applause.—[*Bee*.]

National Intelligencer, 29 September 1818

Andrew Jackson's 1828 election to the presidency represented a political and cultural turning point in American history.[1] Though social trends associated with the Jacksonian era, especially Americans' concern with equality and reform, grew from changes in both industry and government, they were personified in the new president. Jackson scholar Robert Remini writes, "All of it—the excitement, the ferment, the rapid institutional changes—seemed to come together in the person of General Andrew Jackson, the Hero of the Battle of New Orleans. He symbolized this age, both its positive and negative aspects, its democratic spirit and its driving and greedy ambition."[2]

The new nation experienced vast changes. Industrialism transformed the economy; territorial expansion spurred rapid, even chaotic, growth in the West; the birthrate dropped; and the standard of living rose. But the most striking trend was the strengthening of egalitarianism, the notion that America should be a nation of equality. And though large groups of Americans—women, African Americans, and certain immigrant groups such as Irish and German Americans—still lived in a society that was largely unequal, egalitarian rhetoric was so strong that contemporary Europeans "clearly took egalitarianism to be the hallmark of American society."[3] The political process became more inclusive, with increased suffrage for white men, including the elimination of many voting restrictions, and the emergence of campaign techniques designed to win the support of new voters.[4] Jackson's election also brought more popular participation in the inauguration process.[5] And Harry L. Watson argues that the Jacksonians, while supporting only the inclusion of white men in the democratic process, "laid the rhetorical groundwork for a much broader conception of 'the people' in the future, against the resistance of a much more exclusive opposition."[6]

American ideas about who should be worthy of full citizenship experienced a true metamorphosis. And this new sense of the worth of an individual citizen permeated into other aspects of American lives. Newspaper obituaries, as both record and commemoration, reflect individual attributes in this pivotal era and provide a window to explore some of the intricacies of the new, more egalitarian nation. The characteristics of Americans published and legitimized in obituaries provide evidence that cultural values changed and, indeed, became more inclusive in nature, but because of social resistance to total equality, those characteristics were also influenced by race, class, and gender.[7]

The National Newspapers

Because inclusion does not change overnight, this chapter examines characteristics of Americans in 658 obituaries in 1818 and 1838, ten years before and after Jackson's election to the presidency, a pivotal historical event. The obituaries appeared in *Niles' Weekly Register* in 1818, *Niles' National Register* in 1838, the *National Intelligencer* in 1818, and the *Daily National Intelligencer* in 1838, publications that were national in scope and were among the most prominent and influential mass publications of the era. *Niles' Weekly Register* (later *Niles' National Register*), a forerunner of the modern news magazine, was published from September 1811 through September 1849 as a nonpartisan political weekly. Media scholar Frank Luther Mott heralds it as the "chief reliance of the historiographer for the first half of the nineteenth century."[8] The publication's founder, Hezekiah Niles, included obituaries but warned readers in 1821 that he would make available little space for notices of the passing of private individuals.[9] Public figures, he believed, were more worthy of commemoration. Mott calls the *National Intelligencer,* which published from 1800 to 1865, the "first of the important papers in the new capital, and in some respects greatest of the long line of national papers."[10] In his history of the newspaper, William E. Ames credited the long life of the *National Intelligencer* (later called the *Daily National Intelligencer*) to its "high journalistic standards, quiet dignity, and the strong intellectual character."[11] Copied by other newspapers long before cooperative news gathering services such as the Associated Press, the *National Intelligencer* was the closest America had to a national newspaper. The paper seemed to have fewer limits on publication of death notices and included numerous obituaries of men, women, and children from throughout the nation.

The American press experienced a boom in the latter part of the eighteenth century and the early nineteenth century. The number of newspapers increased from thirty-five weeklies in 1783 to 1,200 weeklies and dailies in 1833.[12] Publications during this era were mostly political in content and appealed to middle-class literate citizens who were increasingly looking for domestic rather than foreign news.[13] As a result of passage of the Post Office Act of 1792, newspapers could send issues to each other free of charge, a process that worked as an informal news service.[14] Because of this practice, editors could choose obituaries from other publications and publish them verbatim, thereby giving broader public attention to the deaths of individual citizens.

Politically, while the nation valued more the "common man" during the Jacksonian era, by the 1830s the press was on the verge of a revolution that would give that common man an affordable daily newspaper. But although the first major penny newspaper caused a stir in New York as early as 1833,[15] most papers in the 1830s still remained relatively small and aligned with political parties for both economic support and circulation. These newspapers affected the nation's political character, but as this study and others illustrate, they made a broader cultural impact as well.[16]

THE OBITUARY

What did the Jacksonians consider to be an obituary? Early- to mid-nineteenth-century American dictionaries defined *obituary* as "a register of deaths" or an "account of the deceased," thus including both a chronicle of deaths and a commemoration of what was deemed worthy of remembering about individual lives.[17] Obituaries in the *National Intelligencer* typically were anchored on page 3 under headlines reading "Deaths," "Obituary," or "Longevity" (if the deceased was advanced in years). *Niles' Weekly Register* published obituaries in various locations, sometimes on the front page and sometimes inside in sections labeled "Chronicle" or "Miscellaneous." Although there was no standard headline, presses at that time could not cross columns, the format for the periodical's death notices was fairly consistent and usually began with "*Died*," the name of the deceased, or "*Longevity*."[18] Revolutionary veterans often were singled out with separate lead-ins such as "*Another!*" Both publications frequently reprinted obituaries published in other newspapers, and, as indicated either by a signature initial or the small headline "communicated," many of the obituaries were likely written by contributors rather than by the newspaper editors.

1818

Boone's Premature Demise

In 1818, ten years prior to Andrew Jackson's presidential election, editors at *Niles' Weekly Register* seemed to recognize an obituary's potential contribution to public memory. The periodical published on 19 September an erroneous recounting of the death of Daniel Boone, who supposedly "breathed out his last" in a deer lick "with gun in his hand just in the act of firing." "As he lived so he died," the obituary noted.[19] However, on 7 November the periodical retracted the obituary, calling it a "fabrication," and on 26 December *Niles'* published a longer explanation, saying the fabrication was "probably framed for the purpose of introducing the fanciful incident of the heroic woodsman, breathing his last with his cheek pressed against the butt of his favorite rifle."[20] The editors may have seen the potential for Boone's false obituary to contribute to a frontier legend that could have manipulated public memory with its commemoration of a hero.

Memories of other citizens not as famous as Boone also served as public examples of a worthy life, a type of guide in 1818. The *National Intelligencer*'s obituary for industrious, kind, and amiable lawyer James B. Lane, "who was remarkable for avoiding everything like dissipation," said, "May his life be an example, and his death prove a warning voice, to the young, the thoughtless, the gay, and the dissipated."[21] Paul Carrington's "character and services to his country," another obituary said, "entitle him to the grateful remembrance, and perfect respect of those who knew him."[22] And the fact that Dr. Richard C. Dale's company did not lose a man in 1809 (while camped in a particularly dangerous spot near New Orleans) was recounted in his obituary, not merely as an interesting anecdote: "It is useful to record this fact," his obituary noted.[23]

In 1818 men were more visible than women as examples to be

commemorated: in that year, *Niles' Weekly Register* published forty-three obituaries, including thirty-eight men (88 percent) and five women (12 percent), and the *National Intelligencer* published 197 obituaries, including 143 men (73 percent), forty-seven women (24 percent), and seven children or teenagers (3 percent). Military service was by far the most prominent occupation for men in these notices, with military service outranking public office by more than two to one in the *Intelligencer* and nine to one the *Register.* In fact, no *Register* obituary listed only the public offices held by the deceased without listing his military record as well, and political parties were not mentioned. Of the 143 men eulogized in the *Intelligencer,* only twenty had occupations other than military service or public office, including doctors, ministers, a mason, a bank cashier, a hairdresser, a surgeon's mate, merchants, academics, a newspaper editor, a printer, a museum proprietor, and planters. Obituaries in the Republican-sympathetic *Intelligencer* in 1818 occasionally referred to party affiliation. Neither publication listed occupations outside the home for women, who were nearly always identified by their associations with husbands, fathers, sons, or brothers. Scholars have pointed out that some women of the era were partners or assistants in their family businesses, others ran preindustrial cottage-based industries, and still others were teachers.[24] Were these women who died in 1818 not employed, or were their occupations simply not worth remembering in a published obituary?

Heroes of the Revolution

ANOTHER REVOLUTIONARY PATRIOT GONE!

Lately, at Camden, S.C., Col. JOHN CHESTNUT, in the 78th year of his age. This venerable citizen was distinguished by his zeal and patriotism in the service of his country throughout the revolutionary war, and contributed not a little to the success of the eventful struggle for American Independence.

National Intelligencer, 9 May 1818

The nation was expanding in 1818, but although obituaries revered the pioneer-adventurer, as indicated by the Boone hoax, it was not the most dominant symbol associated with American public memory in obituaries. That designation, an element of media framing through selection and emphasis, went to the revolutionary patriot. Participation in the American Revolution, still part of the remembered American national experience in 1818, was listed in half of the male obituaries in the *Register* and in twenty-eight of the *Intelligencer*'s death notices. In both publications, service to country during the war for American independence was mentioned more frequently even than religious affiliation. Sometimes, revolutionary service was the only attribute listed.[25] Other obituaries told of bravery and gallantry in specific battles, and six men in *Niles* and two in the *Intelligencer* were called heroes because of their patriotic service.[26] Following the obituary of patriot David Humphries, "one of the best men that ever lived," the *Register* lamented that in a few years, there would be no revolutionary patriots left for posthumous notice: "Still the consolation is left that so many have lived to see such glorious fruits from their toils, privations and hazards, and to behold their country rapidly getting the bone of manhood, respected abroad, and happy at home, beyond any other on the globe."[27] Patriotism displayed in other wars was important, too, though not as often mentioned. The only 1818 obituary obviously written for a non-Caucasian remembered the life of Cherokee Richard Brown, whose character "as a brave chief and gallant warrior" during the Creek war had not been excelled "by any aborigine." "His demeanor on all occasions was such as to ensure the full confidence of his General, together with his personal friendship." A "very numerous and respectable assemblage" attended Brown's funeral.[28] Adherence to the social order and association with the white leader in war made Brown's life an object of value for public commemoration.

The Icon, George Washington

Any kind of association with George Washington was worthy of mention in 1818 obituaries as well. Benjamin Walker was listed as an aide-de-camp and friend to Washington, and as Walker's obituary stated, that relationship was "epitaph enough. Would you add more?"[29] Another notice described at length the amicable relationship between Patrick O'Flinn, who kept a public house, and Washington, a frequent visitor: "It was remarked on a certain occasion, by one of the gentlemen in Washington's suite, that in all his journeys with the president, he had never seen him so much at home, in a public house, as in captain O'Flinn's, or ever met a man with whom he discoursed *more* familiarly than with him. There were few men with whom Washington was *familiar*."[30] The essence of this seventy-year-old man's life, as recorded in his obituary, was that he was honest, served in a war nearly forty years earlier, and had an amicable relationship with the usually reticent Washington, a major symbol in American public memory.

Pioneer-Adventurer

The pioneer-adventurer was another important icon in the nineteenth century,[31] as several obituaries in both publications reflected. Perhaps the most prominent was for General George Rogers Clark, called in both publications the "Father of the Western Country," a conqueror of the old Northwest during the Revolutionary War. The *Intelligencer* reprinted Clark's obituary from the *Kentucky Register*, which painted this picture of his adventures: "With this little band of Spartans he is seen piercing the gloom of the sequestered forests, illuminating them in quick succession with the splendour of his victories and early inviting his countrymen to a residence his courage and skill had purchased for them."[32] Judge Bennet Searcy, too, was listed as being "among the first settlers" of Tennessee and "one of those who braved all the dangers of Indian depredation to reclaim it from a wilderness."[33] These men were placed on a pedestal in a nation just building its stories of the frontier. Finally, both publications printed an obituary for a man whose first name was unknown but who fit the "adventurer" mold. A "Mr. ——— Lilly," said to have died at the advanced age of 115, was compared with Boone as a settler who supported himself as a hunter "chiefly by his gun." And as both obituaries for Lilly noted, "It is worthy of remark that this very old man never owned or had a bed in his house."[34] For these publications, Lilly's worth as a symbol of a woodsman, of a frontier figure, and of longevity were more important for his obituary than was an accurate record of his name.

The Brave

Personal attributes most often listed in male obituaries were associated with nation building (patriotism, bravery, gallantry, vigilance, boldness, and merit as an officer) or with service (honesty, skill, industry, devotion to duty, public esteem, ardor, integrity, good sense, and zeal). Some, though fewer in number, were associated with relationships, such as hospitality, benevolence, kindness, and gentlemanly deportment. Only rarely were attributes of a good father and husband mentioned.[35] And only once in 1818 was the idea of equality mentioned. David Mitchell, a revolutionary patriot, was described as "noble," but, as his obit ironically assured, "*Liberty and equality* was his maxim."[36]

The American Woman

DIED

In Cumberland, State of Maryland, on the 31st of December, MRS. CHRISTINA MIACHA MAGILL, wife of Mr. Samuel Magill of that town, and daughter of Mrs. Salome Myer, of this city, after an illness of two weeks, leaving an infant daughter of that age, the only living pledge of her affection for a fond husband. In purity of heart—intelligence of mind—mildness of disposition—and suavity of manners—she has left few superiors among her sex.

National Intelligencer, 13 January 1818

Former first lady Abigail Adams was the most famous of the women whose deaths were recorded in 1818. Remembered as "the amiable consort of President Adams" and daughter of the Reverend William Smith, she was described in both papers as an "affectionate, but firm woman" who "had a distinct view of public men and measures and had her own judgment upon them, which she was free to disclose to her friends but not eager to defend in public circles."[37] Though Adams was remembered in part for her vigor, obituaries for most of the other women in 1818 did not extol their firmness of constitution or their political views. Rather, these women were described as patient, resigned, obedient, affectionate, amiable, pious, gentle, virtuous, intelligent, educated, tender, innocent, and useful. Women were much more likely than men to be described in terms of Christian sentiments and innocence.[38] The obituary for Sarah English serves as a good example of what was deemed valuable about the life of a typical woman of 1818: Mrs. English was "as intelligent as she was good. Not at all ambitious of worldly show, she chose to be useful rather than gay. Her domestic concerns were managed with the most admirable economy exhibiting at the same time a degree of comfort and neatness not to be surpassed—that she might give greater extensiveness to her labors of charity. . . . In her family Mrs. English displayed a rare example of domestic virtue. The most perfect peace and harmony constantly prevailed. . . . In the early stage of her disease she gave up all expectations of recovering; she saw the messenger making his stern approaches towards her—she saw him and smiled; for the Christian, while on the precipice of death, rests peaceful and calm."[39] As a reflector of cultural values, obituaries show distinct differences in society's expectations of men and women in 1818.

Cause of Death

Died—on the 5th ult. At the *nunnery* of Nazareth, in Bardstown, (Ky.) Mrs. *Eleanor Howard*, in the 108th year of her age, without any perceivable sickness.

Niles' Weekly Register, 20 June 1818

Cholera was the most common epidemic to strike during the early 1800s, though scattered outbreaks of yellow fever and smallpox also devastated Americans, especially in cities.[40] However, few obituaries in 1818 listed a specific cause of death other than a painful and long (or lingering) illness, a short or few-days illness, or a severe sickness. Many of these illnesses were "borne without a murmur" or were "endured with Christian patience." Eleanor Howard died at age 108 without any perceivable sickness, and Christopher Greene, former governor of Kentucky, died "after a lingering illness and long protracted bodily excruciations."[41] Notices that did give some details about causes of death did so to explain the untimely death of a person presumed to be healthy or gave details of unusual accidents, such as the death of a elderly man attacked by a bull or the death of a ship's captain washed out to sea and lost.[42] One obituary recounted a death from a wound the man had received in a duel.[43] Editors deemed it necessary to explain why they gave more specific information about the death of an eight-year-old who choked on a stopper from a small chestnut whistle: "We think it proper to subjoin the following facts, connected with this death, for the information and benefit of the public."[44] The newspaper, however, also published on the same day a lurid account of a man who, after the seemingly successful removal of a troublesome toenail, began uttering uncouth expressions, suffered hallucinations, became delirious, went into a fit like lockjaw, and then "expired without a groan."[45] As evidenced by these accounts, obituaries can also tell historians about news values during a particular era. The obituaries illustrate that although these two newspapers were serious political publications, they were not above occasionally using sensationalism to tell stories of citizens' deaths. Further, the obituaries indicate that editors believed that the information benefited the public and served as lessons or warnings.

The Funeral

Obituaries of 1818 were unlikely to publish information in time to provide an announcement of upcoming burial arrangements or services. Newspapers of this era did not hire reporters, instead relying on word-of-mouth messages, letters, or contributors—often anonymous—for information.[46] Thus, death notices were likely not received in time to provide pertinent details of burial. In fact, only 5 of the 240 obituaries in this sample year gave such information, and all ran in the daily newspaper, the *National Intelligencer,* which was more likely to be able to use it. Both publications, however, included descriptions of funeral services in the obituaries of some prominent citizens, especially those with military or Masonic honors. The *Register* gave long accounts of military funerals, listing honors and even publishing the order of processionals.[47] Pomp and ceremony honoring affluent or prominent citizens were worthy of notice in 1818, as was the assurance that funerals were well attended and that burial was done in a respectful manner.

"Without a Struggle"

Finally, obituaries of 1818 also tried to help readers come to terms with the specter of death through the framing of death imagery. With the exception of one notice, which spoke metaphorically of the deceased being "consigned to the narrow house"[48] (the coffin), death imagery in these obituaries was primarily religious in nature. Citizens who lived exemplary Christian lives were said to welcome life's end, as did Rebecca Lowe: "In the full possession of all her faculties, she took leave of her weeping family with the utmost serenity and composure; exhorting them so to live and die, that they might ere long, join her in those realms of bliss to which her happy spirit was about to take its flight—declaring, that to her there was nothing awful in death; that, when called, she felt ready and willing to obey the summons of her God. She was, indeed, a bright evidence for our most holy religion. Her faith in Christ disarmed death of his sting, and the grave of its victory."[49] Her published obituary gave Lowe the opportunity to serve as evidence or a symbol of piety even after her death.

The *National Intelligencer* published numerous accounts reassuring readers of the mental state of citizens on their deathbeds. Rather than struggling to hold on to life, both men and women who died in 1818 were described as leaving their friends and family and meeting death "without a struggle," "resigned and happy," and "with utmost composure and calmness."[50] The *Register* largely ignored the circumstances of death, focusing mainly on the contributions of life. It did, however, describe the death of General Jedediah Huntington: "Correct in his faith, uniform in his holiness, he has been, in his native state, unexampled in his munificence. He died, as he lived, triumphant in his hopes."[51] Obituaries, far from simply recording the fact of someone's passing, also offered some comfort for the public about the nature of death and the promise of immortality for citizens who lived Christian lives.

Post-Jacksonian Obituaries

On Monday evening last, Major E. J. WEED, Quartermaster of the U.S. Marine Corps—a man of kind heart, a gentleman in manners and principles, a devoted husband, and a true friend.

The friends of the family, and the officers of the Army and Navy, are respectfully invited to attend his funeral today, at 11 o'clock A.M. from the residence of R. M. WHITNEY, west of the Seven Buildings.

Daily National Intelligencer, 7 March 1838

In 1838, ten years after Jackson's election to the presidency, newspaper obituaries reflected some distinct changes in citizens deemed worthy of commemoration. But the obituary's potential influence on public memory was not lost on the editors of the *Daily National Intelligencer* and *Niles' National Register* in 1838, just as it had not been in 1818 for *Register* editors who retracted Boone's fabricated obituary. Twenty years later, the notice of the death of William P. Custis (as mentioned in chapter 1) advised readers, "There is in the life of a noble, independent and honest man something so worthy of imitation, something that so strongly commends itself to the approbation of a virtuous mind, that his name should not be left in oblivion, nor his influence be lost. And while we may not speak of him in terms of adulation and undeserved encomium, we may preserve the recollection of those virtues which made him an ornament to society."[52] Custis's life, then, was to serve as a public model, but the man himself was said to be undeserving of adulation. His worth to an egalitarian society was to promote the virtues of everyman, not to be placed on the pedestal of a hero; his character, not his actions, were recorded as the essence of his life. Others, too, led lives deemed worthy of public instruction. Evidence of the influx of immigrants began creeping into newspaper obituaries from 1838, and at least some of these new citizens served as examples. Readers of the *Register*, for example, were told that entertainer Lorenzo Daponte's "memory will endure" and that Americans should be indebted to the Italian immigrant "for the taste everywhere diffused in our country for the music and language of his native land."[53] Daponte's life was commemorated for its positive influence on the community.

1818	**Men**	**Women**	**Children**
National Intelligencer	73 percent	24 percent	3 percent
Niles' Weekly Register	88 percent	12 percent	———
1838			
Daily National Intelligencer	42 percent	37 percent	21 percent
Niles' National Register	96 percent	2 percent	2 percent

Increasing Inclusion in 1838

In 1838, Caucasian men were still considered to be most worthy of commemoration, though women were increasing in numbers. In 1838, the *Daily National Intelligencer* published 376 obituaries, including 160 men (42 percent), 139 women (37 percent), and seventy-seven children or teenagers (21 percent), while *Niles' National Register* commemorated the lives of thirty-nine men (96 percent), one woman (2 percent), and one child (2 percent). While military and public service were still often listed among male obituaries, other occupations were becoming increasingly important in this era, some sixty years after the Revolutionary War but within recent memory of the War of 1812 and Indian wars. In fact, the *Intelligencer* listed other occupations fifty-one times, military service only thirty times, and public office thirty-three times. The other occupations included clerk, poet, shipbuilder, and doorkeeper, evidence of a newspaper willing to include more, different kinds of people in its obituaries. The *Register*, probably because of its stated policy of not publishing obituaries for private individuals, still frequently listed military service and public office, but the number of other occupations listed jumped from one in 1818 to eight in 1838. In both publications women were still identified by their relationships with husbands, fathers, sons, or brothers. However, the *Intelligencer*, which increased its inclusion of women by 13 percent between 1818 and 1838, did mention one woman's employment as a teacher, saying that her "patience, amiability and intelligence eminently qualified her for the duties of the office" and that "her unobtrusive manners, combined with these, seemed to command the respect and kind attention of all."[54] The *Intelligencer* also published obituaries of two nuns.[55]

The Efficient Patriot

Participation in the American Revolution remained worthy of notice in 1838 (it was mentioned eight times in the *Register* and seventeen in the *Intelligencer*), but there was a distinct change in the way these men were described, the way their life chronicles were framed in the media. Joshua Humphreys, for example, was praised for his "superior intellect" and for building the frigate *Randolph* for the war effort. His obituary closed with a tribute to his character: "His moral character was unimpeachable, his professional character unsurpassed."[56] Dr. John B. Tilden was remembered for being "an active and efficient officer in the war of independence, and was afterwards known as a kind and attentive physician, and a devout and useful Minister of the Gospel."[57] Efficiency, kindness, and usefulness, rather than heroism, were noteworthy attributes of this man's life. Thomas Bradford served during the Revolution as commissary general of the

Pennsylvania Division and printer to the Continental Congress. His obituary noted, "The first was a very important public trust, and proves the high estimation which he was held for integrity and knowledge of business. The second shows that he was favorably known to one of the worthiest bodies of men that ever assembled for the good of mankind."[58] The useful, efficient, even businesslike patriot of 1838 had replaced the hero-patriot venerated in obituaries just twenty years earlier.

The Amiable Adventurer

As another ideal in nineteenth-century American public memory, the pioneer-adventurer appeared in five obituaries during 1838. Captain Charles Gatliff, described as "an early adventurer in Kentucky," was remembered for battles against the Shawnee, his exploits as a spy, and his association with Boone, the egalitarian hero who competed with Washington as an important public figure. Gatliff "was a man of rare qualities; fond of the chase," his obituary noted. "The Indians viewed him as a deadly enemy whom they never could surprise." However, his obituary ended on a softer note: "He was of a penetrating mind, manly, hospitable and kind, and died as he had lived, much esteemed."[59]

One of the nation's most famous adventurers, William Clark, died in 1838, and his obituary was published on the front page of the 15 September *Niles' National Register.* The author of his eulogy assumed that "the history of the pioneer trip of Lewis and Clark is familiar to every reader" and paid tribute to Clark's other public attributes: "Through a long, eventful and useful life, he has filled the various stations of a citizen and an officer with such strict integrity, and in so affable and mild a manner, that, at the day of his death . . . had not a blot to fix upon the fair scroll which the history of his well-spent life leaves as a rich and inestimable legacy."[60] Though the brave adventurer was still highlighted in obituaries, linking memories of individual citizens to important cultural symbols in American public memory, these men were now removed from the elite hero's pedestal and were also remembered for their kindness, usefulness, integrity, and hospitality, traits of any man.

Another American ideal, the poor immigrant who succeeds in business, appeared in the 1838 obituaries, though only once. Alexander Milne, said to be "one of the oldest and wealthiest citizens of New Orleans," was described as a poor Scot who arrived in New Orleans "without a penny, but by dint of industry, energy and strict integrity succeeded in business, won the friendship of his fellowmen and laid the foundations of the large fortune which he subsequently accumulated." The benevolent Milne left his fortune to four asylums for orphan children.[61]

Death of the Christian

Departed this life on Monday, the 30th ultimo, after a short illness of a few days, JULIUS C. UNGERER, a native of Pennsylvania, and eldest son of Rev. J. J. Ungerer, in the 15th year of his age. The subject of this notice was, but a few days back, in the enjoyment of excellent health, but the loss of a fond and devoted brother, whose remains he had just followed to an early grave, superadded to a sudden and violent attack of dysentery, soon severed the ties which bound his spirit to earth, and again united him with the object of his affection and love.

Their parents' hearts may indeed bleed, for their bereavement has been heavy; but there is a solace to be found in the promises of our blessed Redeemer, which subdues all anguish, and banishes all wo.

Daily National Intelligencer, 1 August 1838

Though often not considered as a symbol in the public memory of nineteenth-century Americans, one quality of deceased Americans in 1838 prevailed over either the patriot or the pioneer adventurer. Christianity appeared fifty-four times in this sample year as a prominent feature in obituaries of both men and women, providing comfort for bereaved families in this era after the Second Great Awakening, when, as James J. Farrell explains, American religious denominations "increasingly stressed a loving, beneficent God" and the promise of life after death for Christians.[62] Just as some of their forebears did in 1818, these citizens faced death with Christian patience and resignation, often without a murmur. While alive they participated in acts of Christian charity and openly professed their religious beliefs. One man who was "not a professor of the religion of Christ," was, as his obituary was quick to point out, "a liberal supporter of its institutions."[63] And the notion of a resurrection was often mentioned, with hope that the deceased "was about to exchange a world of sorrow for a Heaven of eternal bliss."[64]

The Everyman

It is with the most sincere and heartfelt regret that we announce the death of *Walter S. Franklin, esq.*, clerk of the house of representatives of the United States. He died of bilious fever on the night of the 20th inst. at Lancaster, Pa., where he was on a visit to his friends. Our acquaintance with Mr. Franklin commenced with the extra session, from which period we have had many opportunities of learning his character, which was adorned with every manly virtue. His frankness, kindness and urbanity made him a general favorite, and his loss will be long and sincerely deplored, not only by those with whom he was connected by official relations, but by the more endearing ties of social intercourse.

Niles National Register, 22 September 1838

Personal attributes listed in male obituaries in 1838 were markedly different from those in 1818. Rather than elite or nationalistic characteristics such as patriotism, bravery, gallantry, vigilance, boldness, or merit as an officer, men were noted for character traits more achievable by every man. Benevolence, intellect, kindness, affection, indulgence, devotion to family, friendliness, manners, cheerfulness, unostentatious hospitableness, and amiability would strengthen friendships and family relationships, while efficiency, courtesy, diligence in business, reverence for law, punctuality, energy, industry, frankness in transactions, usefulness, commercial skills, and firmness of character would serve well in business. William E. Payne was praised for his "noble honesty" in paying off his dead father's debts: "The memory of such an act as this," his obituary noted, "is a rich inheritance, to be transmitted from generation to generation."[65] Several men were venerated for their benevolent or philanthropic contributions to the community, one for the unrivaled qualities of his heart, and another for the happiness and hospitality of his fireside.[66] As a result of values reinforced by the rise in capitalism and industry, the brave, zealous public man of 1818 had given way in large part to the useful, amicable, benevolent, punctual businessman of 1838. In fact, the word *hero* was rarely used in 1838 obituaries.

The Admirable Woman of 1838

[COMMUNICATED.]

Departed this life on the 5th June, at Fort Crawford, (Prairie du Chien,) Wisconsin Territory, in the 22d year of her age, Mrs. GWIN THLEAN MCKISSACK, wife of Lieut. W. M. D. McKissack, U.S.A., and daughter of Lieut. Col. John Green, U.S.A.

This event, preceded by an illness of about six weeks, is deeply afflictive to her attached relatives and numerous friends. Distinguished for whatever is estimable in female character, for amiableness and gentleness, for purity of mind, and for reverence for the principles and duties of revealed religion, her memory will be gratefully cherished by all who were acquainted with her worth. Throughout life a model of virtue, in death she proved the efficacy of Christian faith, and enjoyed the consolations of Christian hope.

Daily National Intelligencer, 5 July 1838

Women of 1838 were less innocent and obedient and were more likely to be admired than those in 1818. But these women, too, were pious, benevolent, humble, devoted to domestic duty, virtuous, gentle, kind, indulgent, amiable, unostentatious, pure hearted, patient, intelligent, modest, unobtrusive, reverent, graceful, dignified, and sweet. Many, like Mary Vincent, were said to provide "a beautiful illustration of the blessed principles of Christianity."[67] Nineteen-year-old Mary Rose's "manners were unassuming, her deportment easy, graceful, and dignified, whilst her heart was eminently benevolent, which rendered her lovely beyond comparison," her obituary stated. "With such qualities she won the admiration and esteem of all who knew her, and has left an impression . . . neither time nor circumstances can efface."[68] The life of a woman of 1838 was to be an example for others, her esteem legitimized in death, chronicled and commemorated in her obituary.

Non-Caucasian Assimilation

Despite the growing sense of egalitarianism, obituaries of obvious non-Caucasians in 1838, like those of 1818, reassured readers of the deceased person's voluntary assimilation into the dominant culture. One young woman, Emeline Elizabeth Morgan, was presented as an example to an entire race and class of people: "This subject of this notice, although a colored person, was known and respected for her piety, her exemplary conduct and the many rare qualities not often to be found among persons of her situation in life, and which secured for her, during her painful illness, the kindest attentions of many of the most respectable ladies in the community. Her death, character and public esteem are worthy of public notice, as an example and incitement to others of her class and color."[69] The obituary for Minto Mushulatubbee, a Choctaw chief, noted that he had received a $150 per annum pension for services rendered to the United States and assured readers that "he was a strong friend of the whites till the day of his death."[70] As illustrated by these death notices, a non-Caucasian's adherence to the prevailing social order made the essence of his or her life worthy of presentation for public reassurance in the mass media. In a society increasingly adapting to new immigrant populations, framing these obituaries as examples of assimilation likely reassured middle-class readers about the new ideal of inclusion.

Value of Children

At his father's residence, on Monday last, the 6th instant, after a short but severe illness, LINDSEY MUSE, jr. In the eleventh year of his age. Thus have a kind and affectionate father and mother been bereft of two promising children in the short space of three days.

Daily National Intelligencer, 13 August 1838

	1818	1838
Men	Patriotism	Benevolence
	Gallantry	Intellect
	Vigilance	Kindness
	Boldness	Affection
	Merit as an officer	Indulgence
	Honesty	Devotion to family
	Skill	Friendliness
	Industry	Manners
	Devotion to duty	Cheerfulness
	Public esteem	Hospitality
	Ardor	Amiability
	Integrity	Efficiency
	Good sense	Courtesy
	Zeal	Business diligence
		Reverence for law
		Punctuality
		Energy
		Industry
		Frankness
		Usefulness
		Commercial skills
Women	Patience	Admiration by others
	Resignation	Piousness
	Obedience	Benevolence
	Affection	Humbleness
	Amiability	Devotion to domestic duty
	Piousness	Virtuousness
	Gentleness	Gentleness
	Virtuousness	Kindness
	Intelligence	Indulgentness
	Education	Amiability
	Tenderness	Unostentatiousness
	Innocence	Pure heartedness
	Usefulness	Patience
		Intelligence
		Modesty
		Unobtrusiveness
		Reverence
		Gracefulness
		Dignity
		Sweetness

Death notices of children, much more prevalent in 1838 than in 1818, were less likely to list attributes of character, though several of the deceased were mentioned as youths "of promise."[71] One eleven-year-old girl, however, was said to have an "amiable disposition and endearing qualities of heart and mind," and a six-year-old boy was noted for bearing his painful illness "with Christian fortitude and resignation."[72] Unlike adults, however, ages of children were often described in terms of years, months, and days rather than just years. In an era when birthrates dropped, the lives of children seemed to hold more value, their deaths more likely to be commemorated in obituary columns.

The "King of Terrors"

The cause of death, another framing category, played a much more prominent role in 1838 obituaries than in those from 1818. Though many people still died of "long and painful" or "short but distressing" illnesses, the specific disease was more often listed in the later obituaries, perhaps because of the increasing number of doctors trained during the era.[73] These causes included influenza, smallpox, pulmonary consumption, pleurisy, scarlet fever, apoplexy, stomach inflammation, dysentery, disease of the heart, intermittent fever, bilious fever, dropsy, and yellow fever. Several accidental deaths were listed among the 1838 obituaries, including one from an explosion, one drowning and one fall from a rooftop, which killed a man whose "body and nerves became enfeebled" and who had "expressed apprehension that he would be an object of pursuit."[74]

Not only did obituaries of 1838 offer more information on causes of death, but they also reflected more a society's fears of death than did obits of 1818. Framing of death imagery, for example, was more vivid, as this obituary illustrates: "The visitations of the great 'King of Terrors' are well calculated to remind us of our mortality, and to warn us to be ready for a never-failing event, over which we can exercise no control. His approaches, at all times, and under all circumstances, excite in every well-regulated bosom the most solemn emotions."[75]

One woman was said to have been "cut down by the strong arm of death and hurried to an early grave," but her obituary was quick to point out that she had "winged her flight to the mansions of eternal repose."[76] Another woman's obituary lamented the brevity of life: "Within the short period of a year she was a bride, a beloved wife and companion, a mother, a corpse! 'Early bright, transient, chaste as morning dew. She sparkled, was exhal'd, and went to heaven.'"[77] Obituaries of 1838 also offered more descriptions of bereavement than did those in 1818. One, for example, spoke of the melancholy brought about by a teenager's death: "Her friends are heavily afflicted by her loss, and her poor widowed mother, almost heart-broken, can scarce support her bereavement. It is with a bleeding heart her virtues are here inscribed."[78] Several obituaries published short, sentimental poems about death and the deceased. Most were for young children, such as the one that introduced the obituary for seven-year-old Mary Berry, who "died after an illness of unexampled suffering":

When blooming youth is snatched away,
By death's resistless hand,
Our hearts the mournful tribute pay,
Which pity must demand.[79]

One of the poems, however, was for a twenty-six-year-old man:

But what avails
the bitter tears we shed
Now hope lies buried
in the silent tomb?
For he, the loved,
the gifted one, is dead,
And friendship weeps
o'er his untimely doom.[80]

So although most people who were commemorated in 1838 still met death with "calmness and resignation" or with "unshaken confidence to the enjoyment of a blessed immortality,"[81] 1838 obituaries increasingly reflected a society more willing to express the pain of death and more sentimental in its recollections of the dead.

Finally, 1838 obituaries were much more likely to run advance notification of services than to describe the pomp and ceremony of a funeral after it occurred. The *Register,* for example, described only four funerals after the fact, including only one long description of a military ceremony and processional.[82] Rather than separating the deceased, obituaries more often emphasized the grief of surviving family members and circles of friends.

Increasing Inclusion

Obituary coverage of Americans in the mainstream press did become more egalitarian in the twenty years surrounding Jackson's election to the presidency. Although women still were likely to be included in 1838 based on their associations with men, their numbers did increase by 13 percent. More men, too, were commemorated in 1838 without being military heroes or known public servants; nonetheless, their lives were deemed worthy of remembering. This new inclusion, however, did not benefit Native Americans or African Americans. If members of these groups were remembered at all, it was for their subjection to the dominant culture.

These commemorations of the lives of individual citizens were intended to serve as examples to the public and to preserve those citizens' virtues for collective memory. Private attributes of these men, women, and children, made public after their deaths, reflected early-nineteenth-century America's changing cultural, political, economic, and social order. By 1838, a citizen could finally be noticed and legitimized with the traits of kindness, integrity, and hospitality.

Men in 1818 were praised for their military prowess, valor, bravery, and gentlemanly qualities. They were even venerated as heroes, as was patriot David Humphries, "one of the best men that ever lived."[83] By 1838, however, obituaries were less likely to put even revolutionary patriots and pioneer adventurers on too high a pedestal, as with the obituaries of the efficient John Tilden and the affable General

William Clark.[84] Rather, men of this era were venerated for more democratic virtues of kindness, business acumen, honesty, integrity, and even punctuality. And finally, the decrease in the descriptions of funeral pomp and ceremony points, too, to the rise in importance of the common man. Attributes of women also changed during the twenty-year span. By becoming less obedient and more admirable, as was nineteen-year-old Mary Rose, who left an impression neither time nor circumstances could efface,[85] these women made strides, though ever so slight, toward equality, with published descriptions of their intelligence, dignity, and benevolence. Women in both sample years were praised for their modesty and unobtrusive nature and for setting a pious standard to be emulated by all women in their communities. Their lives celebrated and safeguarded the ideal of the day.

Changes in obituaries reflect the rising value of the businessman in a nineteenth-century America entering an industrial age and reflect the slipping, though still strong, value of the patriot. In these years following the Second Great Awakening, death notices of both genders point to the strength of Christianity as an ideal in American lives, but the 1838 obituaries reflected a society increasingly reflecting on the last hours of life. Obituaries strove to help citizens cope with this worry through promise of resurrection and reconciliation, as the notice of the death of Eleanor Sprigg instructed in 1838: "We are led to reflection the merits of the dead, to form a more just opinion on the usefulness of virtue, and to learn how to appreciate its undying rewards. . . . It forces us to know that, by the practice of virtue, we shall at length all be reunited in another and a better state of existence, never again to die or be separated."[86] By publishing and thus legitimizing the attributes deemed worthy of the lives of individual citizens, obituaries added to collective memory values associated with both life and death in the Jacksonian era. These death stories, as Joseph A. Amato described, were "made buoyant by metaphor and given meaning by the rituals of culture and promise of religion."[87] These obituaries resonated in American consciousness, showing a society that increasingly valued the everyday citizen—and a society struggling with the loss felt when that everyday citizen met the "King of Terrors."

DEATH IN THE CIVIL WAR ERA

Sudden Death.—About twelve o'clock, on Monday night, Mr. George Ensor died very suddenly at the Mount Clare depot. It appears that the deceased had been in the employ of the Baltimore and Ohio railroad company for about 20 years, and on the night of his death had been attending to his duties as a watchman. When found, he was lying upon the floor with his face downward, and life totally extinct. Coroner Chalmers held an inquest over the remains, and the jury rendered a verdict of death from "a visitation of God." The remains were conveyed to his late residence on Cove street, between Raborg and Fayette. He leaves a wife and children.

Baltimore Sun, 6 June 1855

The Civil War was the most dramatic event of the nineteenth century and arguably remains one of the most important cultural and political influences in American history. America emerged from the war not merely as a confederation of states but as a nation with a strong central government, well entrenched in the industrial era. The post–Civil War political culture found Americans more concerned with the greater community than with that ideal of liberal individualism so important after the colonial period.[1] But in the mid–nineteenth century the right to vote was increasingly linked with the rights of the citizen, and the Civil War not only incorporated the African American male into the political culture but also "introduced two new concepts into constitutional law: the principles of national citizenship and equal protection under the law."[2] The United States was becoming, at least in theory, a more egalitarian nation for men. And though it would be 1920 before women's voting rights were constitutionally secured, Civil War–era rhetoric emphasizing citizen rights helped inspire the postwar movement for women's rights.[3] Obituaries published in major regional newspapers before and after the Civil War indicate increasing inclusion in a nation moving headlong into the industrial age.

The war was a watershed for change, and if national memory in America is strongest when it is needed to aid in conflict or reconciliation,[4] public memory in years surrounding the war should have been strong indeed. In fact, newspaper obituaries of the era offer evidence of that strong national memory in continued references to national icons such as George Washington and other revolutionary patriots.

Culture of Death

Not only did American ideas about citizenship and equality merge during the Civil War era, public notions about death and the dead also experienced significant change. Gary Laderman explores this cultural and scientific evolution by examining the changing status of the corpse in the early nineteenth century—changes that led to the postwar emergence of the funeral industry, "a nationally organized confederation of market-conscious American death specialists" who "assumed a hegemonic position over the dead, and began to serve as mediators between them and the living."[5] Throughout the first half of the nineteenth century, death was "an integrated element of everyday life" with its own "economy of symbols and collective imagination."[6] Laderman writes, "A softer, sentimentalized imagination and religious sensibility developed near the beginning of the nineteenth century. Based in part on the rise of evangelicism . . . , modified religious interpretations of death began to proliferate in northern communities and replace the once-dominant Puritan system."[7] Concern over the fate of the soul helped give sentimental memories of the deceased a place in early-nineteenth-century Americans' collective memory. However, the Civil War, Laderman argues, "diffused the shock value of the corpse and restructured its meaning in ways that were antithetical to notions of sacrifice and regeneration, of triumph and redemption. The barrage of severed limbs, lifeless bodies, and anonymous graves accelerated the turn away from the spiritual significations of the corruptible body and toward a greater admiration for emotional and intellectual detachment from it. . . . Over the course of the Civil War, the adoption of a detached, unemotional attitude toward the physical remains of the dead became a reasonable, some would argue even patriotic, sensibility."[8] Advances in medical science, many inspired by the carnage of war, an increased acceptance of embalming, and changing funeral practices also influenced Americans' attitudes toward their dead. Modern science gained its foothold in the United States between 1846, the year of the founding of the Smithsonian Institution, and 1876, when Johns Hopkins University opened.[9] Doctors were becoming more and more involved in the deaths of Americans, and as citizens increasingly turned over the duty of dealing with the corpse of a loved one to scientists and funeral practitioners, the detachment to the physical aspects of death increased. Though Americans honored the memory of their dead following the bloody Civil War, they no longer focused on the corpse or the act of dying. They turned attention away from the physical aspects of death and, at least in obituaries, toward the values of the individual life. Obituaries in mass-circulation newspapers prior to the Civil War, as reflectors of values, provide evidence of the sentimental and religious aura surrounding death, and following the Civil War reflect this cultural attitude of indifference toward the act of dying.

A Split Nation

Changing notions about death certainly permeated mid-nineteenth-century culture, but they did not divide the nation. The core of era conflict lay in a strong regional split that was both political and cultural in nature. Daniel J. Elazar writes of the struggle, "While the immediate bone of contention dividing the two extremities of the nation was the slavery issue, the roots of their mutual antagonism lay much deeper, embedded in major cultural differences between the Yankees in greater New England . . . on one hand, and the self-proclaimed cavaliers of the plantation South on the other. The fact that these cultural differences were manifested with a common American civilization only served to deepen the intensity with which they clashed."[10] Newspaper obituaries provide still more layers of evidence of these regional cultural differences and struggles, as reflected in traits of nationalism, character, and attitudes toward death.

Characteristics of Americans in 3,670 obituaries published during the first week of each month of 1855 and 1870, five years before and after the Civil War, illustrate how the war years affected collective ideas of what was important about a citizen's life and the controversial notions about who was worthy of citizenship. Obituaries reflected those changes by becoming more inclusive, by portraying, for example, characteristics more attainable by every citizen and by including people previously ignored. Because some values differed by gender during this Victorian era, obituaries reflected attributes most admired in men and women, reflecting their different standings in society. And because regionalism was such a strong influence during this era, obituaries in the South differed from those in the North, offering insight into cultural divisions.

The Newspapers

The *New York Daily Times*, *New Orleans Picayune*, and *Baltimore Sun* were popular and prominent in their respective regions. The *New York Daily Times* (later the *New York Times*) began publishing four pages a day in 1851 as another addition to that city's penny press. It was, according to Frank Luther Mott, unusually well edited and grew with unprecedented speed. By 1860 it had doubled its size to eight pages and had become one of the top circulating newspapers in the city. "Its news was well balanced, well edited and copious. . . . [I]t had strong opinions and it was fond of controversy," Mott wrote, but it never descended to sensationalist depths as did other New York penny papers such as the *Herald* or *Sun*.[11] It was, in fact, the only New York penny paper to survive.

The *New Orleans Picayune*, credited with pioneering modern war correspondence, was also known for its wit, cleverness, and use of the telegraph.[12] "The paper became the official journal of New Orleans on May 11, 1854, a tribute to its increasing influence, as was the awarding of the post-office contract," which went to the newspaper with the largest proved circulation.[13]

Founded in 1837, the *Baltimore Sun* prospered almost immediately and has been noted for its enterprise reporting and its use of the telegraph.[14] During the war, the *Sun* operated under duress in this border city, which experienced mob violence and lengthy military occupation. Although the *Sun* was a Southern sympathizer, the paper, in an effort to outlive the upheaval, adopted a policy of silence regarding wartime political issues. By the end of the war, eight Baltimore papers folded, but the *Sun* managed to survive.[15]

Changes in Journalism

Journalism itself was experiencing a metamorphosis during the Civil War era. Newspapers had begun hiring reporters to gather news, rather than relying on other newspapers, personal letters, and gentleman contributors, and the war elevated the status of those reporters. New technology, specifically the telegraph, gave the news a sense of urgency and made brevity more of an industry rule. And thanks to the penny press revolution, newspapers in the mid–nineteenth century were less partisan, gearing themselves to a mass audience rather than an elite political minority. As a result, the *Times*, *Picayune*, and *Sun* published significantly more obituaries for ordinary citizens than did 1818's and 1838's *Niles' Weekly Register* and *Daily National Intelligencer*, which focused on those who were in the military or public service (see chapter 2).

All three of these Civil War era newspapers published, under the headline "Deaths" or "Died," lists of short death notices that included basic information about the deceased such as age, place of death, cause of death, occupation, and funeral arrangements. These briefs occasionally listed attributes of the deceased or bits of religious verse. They were published adjacent to advertising columns, and there is evidence that families were charged a fee for publication.[16] Longer obituaries published within or beside these columns often listed attributes of the deceased and sometimes expressed religious sentiment. These pieces occasionally were signed with initials, indicating that family members or friends may have been the authors. In addition to these brief death listings, the papers published obituaries in their news columns for prominent newsworthy citizens and were less likely to include religious rhetoric or sentimental verse. These obituaries did, however, list the person's attributes and community contributions. All publications frequently reprinted obituaries published in other newspapers, and many indicated that the information was received by telegraph. The interview was an emerging news-gathering technique of the era, but none of the obituaries published in the sample weeks included interviews, a news style found in the twentieth century. Though the news obituaries carried no signatures or bylines, differing writing styles would indicate that some of them, too, might have been submitted by the public as well as written by reporters.

1855

A Public Record in 1855

Editors at the *New York Daily Times* in June 1855, in this era of great political strife, published an article to rebut obituary information published in "Western slavery papers" about the amiable and inoffensive character of Malcom Clark, a proponent of slavery: "It is well enough to understand what these Western Missourians, who vote in Kansas, understand by 'amiable and inoffensive,'" the anonymous author wrote. "A few years ago [Clark] would kick his wife when angry. . . . I need not add that he was a drunkard."[17] It was important for *Times* editors to set the public record straight about the deceased's character to prevent his obituary from influencing public opinion as well as inspiring emulation.

Surprisingly, however, only one *Times* obituary in the sample weeks in 1855 referred to sectional strife. Jesse Chickering was called one of the "profound thinkers and writers on the Slavery question." His views, according to this eulogy, would eventually come into favor and be "largely quoted," enabling him to "receive due honor."[18]

During the twelve weeks examined in the *New York Daily Times* in 1855, five years before the outbreak of civil war in America, 528 death notices and forty-nine longer news obituaries were published. Of these news obituaries, forty-five (92 percent) commemorated the lives of men and only four (8 percent) were for women. Listings of "Deaths" were 38 percent men, 34 percent women, and 28 percent children under eighteen, with the percentage of women up 3 percent from the *Daily National Intelligencer* of 1838. Women's lives, then, were considered significantly less "newsworthy" than men's lives in 1855, though their lives were still commemorated in "Deaths" columns, where information was more likely to have been supplied by families and where space might have been purchased. Women's lives, then, seem to have been valued more among family members than newspaper editors.

The Revolution and General Washington

THE LAST OF THE HEROES OF BENNINGTON GONE.

Capt. SIMEON HICKS, the last of the Americans who were in the battle of Bennington, says the Troy *Budget*, died at the residence of his grandson, MAYNARD KNIGHT, in Sunderland, Vt., on Wednesday, the 24th instant, aged 99 years, 5 months and 2 days. He was born in Hobarth, Mass., August 22 1755, and was the eldest of twenty-two children by his father, who was twice married. Capt. H. Served in the revolutionary army at two or three different stages of the struggle—first under WASHINGTON at Cambridge, and afterwards under

STARK in 1777. He participated in all the struggles of the 16th of August, at Bennington, (Hoosick,) to the final and complete discomfiture of the British. During the greater part of that day he was in the front ranks, and in the hottest of the fight. At critical moments, STARK'S position was near his company; many of his comrades were shot down—among others, his right hand man. He was married in 1778 to a daughter of Capt. CONSTANT BARNEY, of Concord, N.H., and after the close of the war settled in Sunderland Vt., where for more than sixty years he maintained the character of an industrious, honest and respectable citizen. Capt. H was a remarkable man physically; for seventy years he had no experience of bodily ailment, and his death and extreme old age was not attended by suffering or pain. Vitality and consciousness gradually left him, so that the moment of his final departure was hardly perceptible. He remains have had a quiet burial among the Green Mountains, but had he lived and died in one of our metropolitan cities they would have been ostentatiously interred in the presence of thousands, and amid military parade and display.

New York Daily Times, *3 February 1855*

Participation in the American Revolution was worthy of notice in obituaries of 1855 in the *Times*, as was any connection with Washington and the founders of the nation. For example, Conrad Bush, despite the fact that he lived to be 102, was noted only for his service in the Revolution, his "personal acquaintance" with Washington, and the fact that he lived on land "received from the Government for services rendered his country" during the war.[19] A man who served under Washington, Simeon Hicks, was called a hero in his obituary, which reassured readers that although his remains were buried quietly in the Green Mountains, "had he lived and died in one of our metropolitan cities, they would have been ostentatiously interred in the presence of thousands and amid military parade and display."[20] Peter Van Antwerp was remembered because he had cast "his first vote for Jefferson," and Sherrine Paulding was noted simply for being the widow and third wife of Major John Paulding, "of revolutionary memory."[21] Jonathan Gillett, "aged ninety-three years and thirty-two days" was remembered in a lengthy obituary for surviving the "wretched condition" of a Revolutionary War prison and for being the oldest inhabitant of his town.[22] In the tumultuous years leading to civil war, nationalism and patriotism were evident in obituaries in this northern newspaper.

Attributes of Men

Men's obituaries in the *Times* in 1855 were likely to list both public and private attributes. Those published public virtues assured obituary readers that the deceased man was highly esteemed, active, intelligent, scholarly, manly, courteous, of strong character, just, honorable, religious (Christian), generous, vigorous, and patriotic. This public man also possessed oratory skills. His more private attributes were modesty, gentleness, integrity, usefulness, hospitality, promptness, energy, honesty, and faithfulness. His worth as a husband and father was also mentioned, and he had a sense of humor. One lawyer was said to have "eccentric habits."[23] Another man, "well known as a monomaniac," was noted for his peculiar religious views, his wandering nature, and his idiosyncrasies, but his obituary was quick to reassure readers that he had lately been "very quiet and laborious, affording great consolation to his family."[24] *Times* editors, though interested in writing about oddities as did many newspapers of that era, were careful to use obituaries to preserve ideal values, not to criticize the deceased for perceived political or social faults.

Women Identified with Men

Characteristics of women portrayed in obituaries published in the *Times* in 1855 were decidedly different from men described in the same sample weeks. Women were remembered for being Christian, gentle, kind, obliging, honest, faithful, beautiful, talented, warm, and happy. Two women were described as being peaceful or calm in death, and one was called an "esteemed servant."[25] Women were most often identified by their associations with men. These relationships with husbands, fathers, or, occasionally, sons and women's value as nurturers were deemed most worthy of commemoration.

Associations

There is evidence in the *Times* in 1855 that men, at least, spent time socializing with groups other than family or church members. An era observer of American society, Alexis de Tocqueville, commented on these groups, arguing that Americans often regarded them as their only means of acting: "Americans of all ages, all conditions, and all dispositions constantly form associations."[26] Though club memberships were not typically listed in the deceased attributes, numerous men's associations published announcements along with obituaries instructing members to attend the funeral of a particular "brother." The groups also often asked members to wear black armbands for thirty days as a sign of mourning. Mentions of these organizations reflect a society concerned with communal associations for enjoyment and for business or social advancement, but memberships in these organizations were not listed as part of citizens' worthy attributes.

Occupations

Men's occupations in *Times* obituaries were in the areas of military, business, public service, and religious communities and reflect a growing emphasis on technology. The obituaries studied included eight clergymen, six merchants, three judges, two naval officers, an infantryman, a newspaper editor, two railroad engineers, a railroad president, an attorney, an army general, a cabinetmaker, an editor, a member of the U.S. Senate, a state legislator, an author of statistical research, a telegraph operator, and a physician. Women were noted for being wives or daughters, but surprisingly, motherhood was not mentioned. For both genders, with the exception of those in service to country or to God, those worthy of a *Times* obituary were typically upper middle class.

The Unusual and Inclusion

A COLORED MAN FELL DEAD.

Yesterday morning Coroner O'DONNELL held an inquest at No. 69 Hudson-street, on the body of a respectable colored man named THOMAS HENRY SONGAN who died very suddenly, and rather mysteriously. He was employed as a steward of the packet-ship *Saint Donn's*, and while attending to a collation on board he was attacked with an affection of the heart—was immediately conveyed home, and when entering the premises, fell to the floor a corpse. The case was thoroughly investigated and the Jury rendered a verdict accordingly. Deceased was aged 32; a native of Delaware.

New York Daily Times, 4 May 1855

An unusual cause of death sometimes encouraged editors to publish news obituaries for different kinds of citizens, including, in these sample weeks, a woman and an African American man. Thomas Henry Songan "fell to the floor a corpse" after an affectation of the heart on board a packet ship where he was employed as a steward. Songan was described as "a respectable colored man" and a native of Delaware.[27] Margaret Morrell was preparing dinner when a cinder snapped out of the fire and caught the handkerchief around her neck on fire. She died from effects of the burn in the "house she occupied for a quarter of a century at least."[28] News values as well as cultural values affected *Times* news obituaries in 1855.

Cause of Death

In Brooklyn, at the residence of her father, Roy Samuel E. Cornish . . . JANE SOPHIA TAPPAN CORNISH, aged 20 years, 6 months and 19 days, after a distressing illness of 3 years and 7 months, which illness was attended with idiocy and insanity, the last 114 hours of which time she was unable to take into her stomach one morsel of food.

She will be taken to the Presbyterian Church, (Rev. Mr. Freeman, pastor,) in Prince-at, Brooklyn, at 2 o'clock P.M., on Wednesday, the 7th inst, where funeral services will be performed and thence to the family lot, Greenwood, for interment. The friends of the family are respectfully invited to attend, without further invitation.

New York Daily Times, 7 March 1855

Although cause of death was sometimes mentioned as a "short but severe illness," a "lingering illness," or a "protracted illness," the *Times* in 1855 listed a specific cause of death in many of its obituaries. More people died of consumption (twenty-seven) than of any other cause. Scarlet fever was listed eight times, congestion of the brain seven times, and heart disease six times. Other causes of death included dysentery, hemorrhage of the lungs, bilious fever, congestive fever, yellow fever, paralysis, hydrocephalus, congestion of the lungs, whooping cough, cholera, bronchitis, inflammation of veins, and inflammation of bowels. One listing in the regular "Deaths" column described twenty-year-old Jane Sophia Tappan Cornish's "distressing illness of 3 years and 7 months which . . . was attended by idiocy and insanity; the last 114 hours of which time she was unable to take into her stomach one morsel of food."[29] The fact that this notice appeared in the "Deaths" column rather than a news column is indicative of the apparent willingness of everyday citizens to list causes and descriptions of death in obituaries.

Sentimental Victorian and religious references to death were published mainly in the "Deaths" listings in the *Times* (or in longer obituaries published either within or alongside those columns). For example, this poem was published with the funeral arrangements for one-year-old Jeanie Hall:

She was the sunshine of our home,
An angel to us given.
Just when we learned to love her most
God called her back to heaven.[30]

Nineteen-year-old John Henry Van Sant also was commemorated by a short poem:

My brother is sleeping
He early was called
From the valley of tears
Our sorrows are mortal
With anguish are torn.[31]

And although twenty-year-old Mary Cass could not speak at the time of her death, her obituary assured readers, "We have every reason to suppose that she recognized the call of the Heavenly Father, and thot 'Not my will but Thine be done'; for after gazing on those she loved she closed her eyes softly and breathed her life away in a few moments like a little child going to sleep."[32] Thus Victorian sentimentality, though not typically a news value in the *Times*, was a part of at least some of the obituaries of everyday citizens published in the daily death listings.

In New Orleans

OBITUARY

Departed this transitory existence, on Thursday, August 2, 1855, after a short illness, JAMES M. OLDHAM, aged 26 years, a native of Louisville, Ky.

By this unlooked for and sad event, has the heart of a fond and doating mother, loving and affectionate brothers and sisters, been deluged in the most poignant affliction, and the bright star that shone so brilliantly athwart the horizon of their affection has paled before the mighty Death King, and left in its trackless path, anguish, sorrow and despair.

Away from the home of his youth, far from the aged mother who idolized him, by his gentle and unassuming manner he won the love and friendship of all who knew him; it must be a source of gratification to that mother to know that his every want was satisfied, his every wish fulfilled. While the brother who laved his heated brow—when the volatile mind, soaring back to the days of his childhood, and slighting in the sepulchre of some childish companion, held sweet with playmates long since dead—wept, when it returned to his mother, and felt stronger in his duty.

Denied that mother's parting kiss, or a sister's soothing word, he bore his sufferings with a patience worthy of an angel; and as the gentle breath of morn wafts into life and beauty the drooping flower, so went his spirit to its God, gently, imperceptibly.

Truly, how evanescent is life. 'Twas but yesterday we greeted him in all the pride of manhood; now he sleeps in eternal night. The hand that in life had often grasped in friendship his many friends, is now clenched with the last conflict; the eye that so often irradiated his intellectual countenance, is now rayless in its indented socket; and the warm and gushing heart, that was "open as day to melting charity," is forever hushed 'neath the humid cerements of the tomb.

But why should we grieve? The voice that had oft enchained the listening stars, and made the stranger linger as the breath of evening bore it to his ear, now swells Heaven's entrancing choir, and once again hath its portals opened to usher in a pure and spotless soul.

Farewell, James, you shall ne'er be forgotten; and while memory continues to treasure on its table all that is noble and just, will you be remembered, while I meekly approach thy tomb and offer this feeble tribute to be entwined in the garland woven to thy memory. S***** M****

New Orleans Picayune, 4 August 1855

In the South, sectional strife or slavery was not mentioned in any of the obituaries published in the *New Orleans Picayune* during the first week of each month in 1855. During these sample weeks, the *Picayune* ran 170 death notices and fifty-two longer news obituaries. Forty-nine men (94 percent) and three women (6 percent) were commemorated in the news obits. Listings of "Deaths" were 25 percent women, 55 percent men, and 20 percent children under eighteen. Thus, the percentage of women commemorated in the New Orleans newspaper's "Deaths" listings was significantly smaller than the 34 percent published the *New York Times* during the sample weeks. Just as in the *Times*, men's deaths were more newsworthy.

The Icon George Washington

Participation in the American Revolution was mentioned twice in obituaries in this southern newspaper, though, unlike *Times* obituaries, revolutionary service was not the only attribute listed. The Reverend John Bryson, for example, was noted not only for his stint in the revolutionary army but for his ministry and his study of theology.[33] Seth Tucker was remembered not only for his revolutionary duty but for being one of the earliest settlers of his community.[34] Any connection with Washington, however, was fodder for an obituary, no matter how vague that connection. Mary Channell was eulogized in a front-page news obituary simply for being "one of the choir of singers that welcomed Gen. Washington upon his visit to

Boston."[35] Thus, Washington prevailed as a patriotic symbol in public memory in both the North and the South.

Gentleman Attributes

The *Picayune*'s attributes for citizens resembled those published in the *Times*. Men were most often noted for public attributes. In 1855, they were highly esteemed, amiable, generous, intellectual, educated, gallant, talented, manly, and courteous. However, men in the *Picayune*, unlike those in the *Times*, were often remembered for being "true gentlemen," and patriotism was not mentioned. Other male attributes listed in the *Picayune* included social qualities such as affection, modesty, graceful humor, boyish manners, simplicity, kindness, and earnestness. Attributes that would serve the community were important, too, such as usefulness, bravery, energy, integrity, ardor, respectability, excellence of character, patience, and perseverance. Men in the *Picayune* were also noted for health and calmness in the face of death. One man was said to have a mind "occasionally clouded with fits of morbid gloominess," but his obituary assured readers that his character was one of "true manly honor."[36] The *Picayune*, too, was slow to use its obituary notices to criticize faults; rather, obituaries commemorated attributes reflecting the ideal. And like in the *Times*, members of men's associations were often asked to attend funerals and wear badges of mourning.

Christian Women

Women whose obituaries were published in the *Picayune* in 1855 were noted most often for their Christianity, goodness, loving nature, amiability, kindness, gentleness, and piety. Also mentioned were a woman's readiness to relieve distress, the fact that she spoke no ill, patience, resignation, calm in the face of death, affability, vivacity, beauty, modesty, intelligence, and excellence as a wife. Again, women were most noted for their nurturing relationships with husbands and fathers.

Unlikely Inclusion

Longevity was more likely than an unusual cause of death to warrant a spot for an unlikely obituary in a *Picayune* news column. For example, on 3 October 1855, the newspaper included a notice for Victorie Simon Mercier, "a colored woman who died yesterday in a house on Royal Street" who had "reached the patriarchal age of 111 years." As her obituary noted, "she remained active and sensible to the last. On Friday last she walked a distance of three squares."[37] Likewise, Native American Buffalo Chief, head of the Chippewa nation, was noted because he died at age one hundred, had "rare integrity, wisdom in council, power as an orator, and magnanimity as a warrior." His obituary reassured readers that he had received the baptismal rites of the Roman Catholic Church.[38]

The Elite

Just as in the *New York Daily Times*, men whose obituaries appeared in the *New Orleans Picayune* in 1855 were likely to be white and upper middle class. Two plantation owners–planters were mentioned, as were four clergymen, four congressmen, three prominent merchants, two judges, two naval captains, two state legislators, and two writers. Other occupations listed fell into the categories of military, including a soldier and infantry captain; public service, including a governor, university president, district attorney, lieutenant governor, deputy sheriff, and auditor of the state treasury; business or private sector, including a bookseller, attorney, railroad engineer, newspaper editor, railroad president, and printer; and ministry, including one missionary. Citizens of color or those in lower economic classes were rarely included, though obituaries often mentioned the deceased's Irish or German heritage. The *Picayune* did publish at least one news obituary of a member of a lower class whose family was left financially bereft by his death. Redmond Ryan, "a delineator of Irish characters and the singer of Irish songs[,] is no more," the obituary noted. "He was a man of no inconsiderable talent and much esteemed for his amiable character and social qualities."[39]

Sentimentality and Death

Causes of death listed in *Picayune* obituaries in 1855 closely resembled those in the *Times*. However, two years after a major yellow fever epidemic in the city, that disease was the leading cause, with thirteen mentions; followed by consumption, "that most insidious and deceptive enemy of man," which was mentioned seven times; and apoplexy and cholera, which appeared four times each.[40] Other causes listed were pneumonia, typhoid fever, chronic bronchitis, flux, congestive chill, stroke, and inflammation of the bowels. One soldier was killed by the premature explosion of a cannon, and a writer was killed by an "accidental bullet."[41] The *Picayune*, unlike the *Times*, often mentioned specific times of death, down to the half hour, focusing still more attention on the act of dying. And in fact, the *Picayune* was much more likely than the *Times* to indulge in sentimentality and religious rhetoric in both news obituaries and those that ran either in or alongside the listings of deaths of everyday citizens—perhaps because of the stronger informal integration of religion into daily life in the traditional South.[42] Obituaries used metaphors—powerful media framing devices—and spoke of deceased men and women as being suddenly removed by the "Omnipotent Author," "scathed by the wing of the destroying angel," "paled by the mighty Death King," or "torn from our midst by the fell destroyer."[43] Sometimes they served as grim warnings. Laura Grace Hyatt's obituary said, "Poor Laura! thy form lies cold and still; thy voice is hushed forever and we bid thee a sad farewell. . . . It was but a few days ago she joined us in our pleasure and but a few days ago her gentle voice mingled with us in our little choir; but she is gone to mingle with the choir in Heaven. To her bereaved family it should be a consolation that she died trusting in her Savior; and to us, her young friends, it should warn us, that life is fleeting, 'We bloom today, tomorrow die.'"[44] An obituary published in a news column described a funeral by saying, "All that was mortal of Francis T. Porter was followed to 'the place appointed for all living' yesterday afternoon by a large number of our most respectable citizens, the friends, acquaintances and associates of the deceased."[45] The *Picayune* might have listed specific medical reasons of deaths for its New Orleans readers, but its obituaries spent much time and space assuring those readers that the true times and causes of deaths were in the hands of the Almighty.

A Border City

Obituaries in the *Baltimore Sun*, published in a border city, reflected male and female attributes and causes of death common to both the northern *New York Daily Times* and the southern *New Orleans Picayune*. In 1855, the *Sun* published 150 news obituaries, including 120 (80 percent) for men, twenty-one (14 percent) for women, and nine (6 percent) for children under eighteen. Of the 615 death notices or obituaries published adjacent to these columns, 35 percent were men, 30 percent women, and 35 percent children. Editors at the *Sun*, like those at the other two newspapers examined for this chapter, believed adults were more important than children for commemoration in news columns, but people who bought obituary space wanted the deaths of their children publicly announced. Even these announcements, however, rarely included attributes of the deceased, only the cause of death, funeral arrangements, and often bits of sentimental or religious verse. The *Sun*'s news columns, however, included significantly more women than did the other two papers—6 percent more than the *New York Daily Times* and 8 percent more than the *New Orleans Picayune*—while still commemorating females in similar percentages in its paid "Deaths" notices. Still, based on a comparisons of the two types of obituaries, the public and family members seemed to have valued women's lives more than did the *Sun*'s editors.

Public Memory in Baltimore

DEATH OF AN OCTOGENARIAN.—Samuel Adams Dorr, Esq., of Boston, died on Sunday last. It is said he was a pupil in the public schools of Boston when President Washington made his Eastern tour, and participated in the services of the occasion.

Baltimore Sun, 1 March 1855

Mention of the American Revolution, Washington, and other symbols associated with national public memory cropped up in obituaries in the *Sun* in 1855, just as in the other two newspapers examined for this study. Like Mary Channell, eulogized in the *Picayune* for singing in a choir during Washington's tour, Samuel Adams Dorr of Boston was remembered in his *Sun* obituary simply for a vague association with the first president. The only identifying information given in his obituary was that "he was a pupil in the public schools of Boston when President Washington made his Eastern tour, and [Dorr] participated in the services of the occasion."[46] A Mrs. Judge Taney was remembered as an "esteemed and beloved lady" and for being "a sister of the late Francis S. Key, the immortal author of 'The Star-Spangled Banner.'"[47] Henry Gassett, one of the oldest merchants in Boston, was commemorated simply as "an intimate personal friend of John Quincy Adams."[48] Mrs. Captain Reed's obituary mentioned her father's service in the Continental Army under Washington and her participation in a group of "young ladies" who, after a new flag design was approved by Congress, "made the first 'star-spangled banner, which was displayed for the first time on the Capital at Washington, on the 13th of April, 1818."[49] Obituaries in the *Sun* in 1855 indeed reflected a strong collective memory of the American Revolution and the founding of the nation, and their content resembled that of *Times* obituaries in their nationalist orientation.

Slavery

The *Sun* might have eventually avoided controversial political coverage, especially about slavery, in news columns during this era, but obituaries in 1855 indicate a definite proslavery slant in coverage of deaths of two citizens. Dolly Robinson, "a colored woman," was remembered in Baltimore for her loyalty to her mistress in Syracuse, New York: "The most remarkable feature of her character was her resolute persistence in maintaining the same relations to her mistress as she held to her Virginia master; so that in spite of the laws of New York—in spite of the peculiar atmosphere of the city of isms, and in the very dust and smoke of the underground railroad, she lived and died in the property of our most excellent and benevolent lady friend."[50] The obituary for the Reverend Dr. William Capers, bishop of a pro-Southern Methodist church that had split with the Methodist General Conference over the issue of slavery, described him as an "eminent divine" and noted that "the church, of which he has been an ornament for many years, has sustained a great loss, and the slave population, over which he had a general oversight, a beloved friend."[51] Thus, proslavery sentiment, all but ignored in the southern *Picayune*, was featured in two front-page obituaries for the edification of the *Sun*'s Baltimore readers in 1855, evidence that the commemorative nature of obituaries might have been exploited to manipulate public opinion.

The Baltimore Man

At his residence in this city, on the 24th of February last, in the 38th year of his age, E. G. HUNICHENN, leaving a wife and three small children to mourn their irreparable loss. The deceased was a native of Germany, but emigrated at an early period of life to this country, and engaged in mercantile pursuits. An affectionate disposition was a distinguishing trait of his character, added to which he was emphatically what the poet describes as "the noblest work of God, an honest man."

His heart was gen'rous, and his mind
Swayed by its guide—Integrity;
In all his dealings just and kind.
His errors claimed our sympathy.
Prompt in feeling, as prompt in deed,
His heart and hand together mov'd;
And when in sorrow or in need,
His friends e'er found how much he loved.
When on his bed of death he laid,
The rising sigh he sought to smother,
And turning to his children, said
"My children, love thy mother."
Here utt'rance failed, and his dim'd eye

Showed life was ebbing from him fast:
Soon pointing upwards to the skies,
With a faint moan, he breathed his last.
Baltimore Sun, 5 April 1855

Men whose obituaries appeared in the *Sun* in 1855 were involved in a variety of occupations, but, as in the *Times* and *Picayune*, most were middle to upper class and fell into the categories of military, public service, business, or clergy. Among the military men were several officers, and public servants included state legislators, judges, congressmen, a former governor, a city auditor, a city councilman, and an auditor of the national treasury. Members of the private sector included newspaper editors, merchants, lawyers, printers, doctors, railroad officials, an inventor, a bank note engraver, a historian, a piano dealer, a head of a calico mill, an edge-tool maker, a bank president, a musician, a hotel proprietor, a machinist, an author, an architect, and a proprietor of a stand of perfumed crystals. Among those in the ministry were several preachers and a bishop of the Methodist Episcopal Church. The few men listed who might not have been of middle-class status were a gas fitter, a mail carrier, and a court clerk. Baltimore men, too, were involved in men's associations such as the Odd Fellows or Masons.

Attributes for men eulogized in the *Sun* during the sample weeks in 1855 resembled those in the other two newspapers. Age or longevity, public esteem, and being well known were the attributes most often mentioned. Many men were noted for public virtues, such as generosity, honor, integrity, intellect, nobility, industry, wealth, munificence, gallantry, philanthropy, heroism, having a democratic spirit, and being eminent, prominent, respected, distinguished, a public man, a champion of education, and a triumphant warrior. Many were noted for private, more social virtues too—kind, gentlemanly, manly, witty, happy, unselfish, popular, a devoted or sincere friend, warm, sober, and a loving father. Some virtues involved religious beliefs, with men described as Christian, pure, and faithful, and others hinted at the importance of business skills, such as competence, usefulness, business talent, enterprise, and support for manufacturing. These obituaries indicate a society that valued strength of character as well as professional accomplishment. Many obituaries also listed native countries of England, Ireland, and Germany, indicating people who wanted to be remembered in part for their European ethnicity.

Women's Attributes in the *Sun*

On the afternoon of the 30th, after an illness of ten days, AUGUSTA, eldest daughter of E. and Julia A. Morrison, aged 19 years and 3 months.

The announcement of the death of this young lady will astonish and shock her numerous friends and acquaintances. Seldom has the declaration that "in the midst of life we are in death" been more suddenly and sadly realized than in her case. A few days since youth, with all its vigor; life, with all that tends to make it pleasant and happy, were hers; now she sleeps in the cold and silent tomb; but "we sorrow not as those without hope." She was ever a most obedient daughter, affectionate sister, kind, gentle and amiable in her disposition, giving every evidence that she was blessed with those christian graces that come only through our Lord and Saviour, Jesus Christ; and a few weeks since, while her prospects for a long life were as bright as the most hale and hearty, she made a public confession of her faith in her Redeemer, and was received into full communion by her pastor. Our kind and merciful God, in his wisdom, deemed it best to remove her from "these lower grounds where sorrows grow" before the troubles and afflictions that fall to the lot of all overtook her; and while we deeply, deeply grieve at our bereavement, we know that our loss is her eternal gain, and with chastened hearts we say, "The Lord gave, and the Lord hath taken away, blessed be the name of the Lord." F.

Baltimore Sun, 4 July 1855

Obituaries for women eulogized in the *Sun* during 1855 closely resembled those in the other newspapers. Most often remembered for their associations with husbands and fathers, they were noted for longevity and for being beloved wives. Their attributes included nurturing traits such as being kind, gentle, affectionate, modest, dutiful, sincere, a devoted mother, meek, innocent, tender, mild, interesting, amiable, and one who made the happiness of her home her greatest worldly care. Some attributes highlighted the physical, with women described as attractive, as having prepossessing features, and as being slender, frail, and lovely.

Some attributes highlighted a woman's religious beliefs, describing her as a devoted Christian, church member, faithful, and having an ethereal spirit. Only a few women commanded respect and were esteemed, excellent, noble, and gifted. Mary G. Horsford was noted for her work as a writer, but even she was identified as the wife of a science professor connected with Harvard University. However, she was also commemorated for her poems, which were "much admired for their easy and correct versification, and for their simple but beautiful imagery."[52]

Specific Causes

The *Sun*, like the *Times* and *Picayune*, sometimes listed causes of death as either short or lingering illnesses but more often gave specific causes of death. They included yellow fever, consumption, drowning, railroad accidents, typhoid fever, heart disease, erysipelas, tooth operation, bowel inflammation, paralysis, arterial hemorrhage of the stomach, severe colds, dysentery, accidental shootings, cholera, injuries suffered in a fall, brain inflammation, brain congestion, liver congestion, strangulated hernia, bursting of blood vessel in the head, congestive fever, scarlet fever, diarrhea, neuralgia, apoplexy, catarrhal fever, smallpox, lung congestion, chronic croup, and lung hemorrhage. The *Sun* had some different types of causes than the other two newspapers, including being shot in a riot, violent cholera morbus from eating green corn, buzz saw accident, rattlesnake bite, being caught in a printing press, being burned in laboratory fire, or being killed by Indians.[53] One man's death was listed, by order of the coroner, as a "visitation of God."[54] Another obituary gave a long, descriptive account of a four-year-old's premonition of his own death in a fire the evening and morning before it happened: "This was a most extraordinary presentiment," his obituary noted, "and during the whole day he spoke of dying though he had enjoyed excellent health. The boy is said to have been a sprightly and interesting child, and was beloved by all who knew him."[55] And still another obituary offers evidence of an interest in the corpse and burial. Harmon Weedon, eighty-six, had made arrangements for his own funeral and had constructed for himself a coffin of Cayuga limestone: "His coffin weighed one thousand five hundred pounds, and he gave particular directions how to lower him into the grave. All of his directions were explicitly followed, and by his directions the coffin was not only bolted, but cemented together, so as to be watertight."[56] As indicated by these specific causes and descriptions of citizens' preoccupations, the specter of death was a persistent part of Baltimore's culture, just as in New York and New Orleans.

Religion and Sentimentality

Though religious rhetoric and sentimentality were rare in news obituaries, they were often included in death notices for which contributors paid. In fact, in the *Sun*, 120 obituaries listed either religious rhetoric or sentimental poetry, and thirty-one included the phrase "Rest in Peace," many more than in the other newspapers examined. The obituary for Harriet McLain, published in the paid "Died" column, said, "This excellent lady had been for many years a consistent member of the Methodist Episcopal Church, and adorned the doctrines of Christ her Saviour.—Throughout a period of several weeks affliction she evinced perfect resignation to the Divine will, and in life's closing scene expressed her desire 'to depart and be with Christ,' exclaiming, in tones of triumph, the words, 'Glory to God! Glory to God!'"[57] And another paid obituary, this one for John Walker, included the following poem:

His languishing head is at rest,
Its thinking and aching are o'er,
His quiet, immovable breast
Is heav'd by affliction no more.
His soul has now taken its flight
To mansions of glory above,
To mingle with angels of light,
And dwell in the kingdom of love.
Then let us forbear to complain
That he has gone from our sight.
We soon shall behold him again,
With new and redoubled delight.[58]

If the *Baltimore Sun* was indeed a Southern sympathizer, as the Emerys argue,[59] evidence that the city resembled its southern neighbors in cultural attitudes about religion and death can be found in these numerous sentimental obituary notices placed by bereaved family and friends prior to the Civil War.

1870
The New York Times

Decline in Sentimentality

Some five years after the Civil War, sentimentality about death was noticeably absent from obituaries published in the *New York Times*. In fact, only one notice sought to romanticize death, an obituary for an elderly Methodist minister.[60] Fifteen years and a long Civil War had made their mark on the commemorations of deceased citizens in 1870: obituaries no longer dwelled on the act of dying or its religious implications—death had become far too familiar. During the twelve sample weeks examined in 1870, the *Times* published 945 obituaries, 417 more than in 1855, including 55 in news columns. News obituaries for men still outnumbered those for women by ten to one, but 40 percent of death notices were for women, 46 percent for men, and 14 percent for children. Women continued to gain in numbers on the *Times*'s obituary pages, at least in the death notices.

1855		**Men**	**Women**	**Children under 18**
	New York Daily Times	92 percent "news"*	8 percent "news"	———
		38 percent "deaths"	34 percent "deaths"	28 percent "deaths"
	New Orleans Picayune	94 percent "news"	6 percent "news"	———
		55 percent "deaths"	25 percent "deaths"	20 percent "deaths"
	Baltimore Sun	80 percent "news"	14 percent "news"	6 percent "news"
		35 percent "deaths"	30 percent "deaths"	35 percent "deaths"
1870				
	New York Times	90 percent "news"	10 percent "news"	———
		46 percent "deaths"	40 percent "deaths"	14 percent "deaths"
	New Orleans Picayune	96 percent "news"	4 percent "news"	———
		51 percent "deaths"	27 percent "deaths"	22 percent "deaths"
	Baltimore Sun	88 percent "news"	8 percent "news"	———
		34 percent "deaths"	32 percent "deaths"	34 percent "deaths"

*"News" obituaries were published as newsworthy items apart from columns of "deaths," which included paid obituaries.

Heroic Service

BURIAL OF A NAVAL HERO
Funeral of the Late J. M. Wainwright,
Master in the United States Navy

The funeral of JONATHAN MAYHEW WAINWRIGHT, late Master in the United States Navy, took place at Trinity Chapel, in Twenty-fifth-street, at 10 ½ A.M., yesterday. The body of young WAINWRIGHT arrived here on

Saturday in the United States steamer *Mohican*, on board which vessel he died on the 19th of June from wounds received on the 17th during an attack on the pirate ship *Forscard* on the coast of Mexico. The full particulars of the engagement in which young WAINWRIGHT lost his life were given in the TIMES of Saturday last, as narrated by the surgeon of the *Mohican*. Both before and after his death-wounds he displayed heroism and bravery worthy of his distinguished sire, Commander J.M. WAINWRIGHT, who lost his life in the service of his country while commanding the *Harriet Lane*, near Galveston, at the beginning of the rebellion. The deceased was the grandson of the late Bishop WAINWRIGHT, and was appointed to the Naval School by President LINCOLN. He was only twenty-two years of age at the time of his death.

The funeral services at the church yesterday were in accordance with the forms of the Episcopal Church and were conducted by Rev. Dr. HIGBEE, assisted by Rev. Dr. SWOPE. Among the naval officers present were Master J. P. Morrill and Midshipmen Chas Briggs, J. J. Hunker, T. G. C. Slater, J. H. Bull and H. B. Tyler.

The mother of the deceased and a younger brother, ROBERT P. WAINWRIGHT, who had just entered the Military Academy at West Point, were the chief mourners—being the only surviving members of the family.

The coffin was of rose-wood, silver mounted, and on the lid was placed the sword of the deceased, environed with wreaths of camellias. No sermon was preached, and after the reading of the burial service, the body was removed from the church, and, followed by the relatives and late comrades of the deceased, was taken to Green Wood Cemetery, where it was deposited in the family vault.

New York Times, 4 August 1870,

Though the *Times* did not romanticize death in 1870, service to country during conflict or war was heralded as heroic and noble. Joseph E. Hamblin, a major-general, was lauded as "One of the most gallant soldiers that fought for the union in the late war, and a gentleman whose character was without a blemish. . . . He was in the final struggles around Richmond, and only sheathed his sword when his country had no further need of his services."[61] Another general, Hiram Walbridge, was remembered for his "prompt and bold stand in favor of the Union" and his work "with tongue and pen, . . .

arousing the patriotism of the people, particularly of the commercial classes."[62] And George H. Thomas, a southern-born general who fought for the Union, was called "a hero among heroes" and was eulogized for five days in long notices about his death, military service, and elaborate funeral.[63] Thus, bravery, patriotism, and public-spiritedness were among the attributes noted in *Times* obituaries for men during the sample weeks examined in 1870.

The American Revolution was still worthy of mention, though the deceased were now sons of revolutionary veterans.[64] A symbolic settler was mentioned, too, in the obituary of Samuel Campbell, said to have descended from "sturdy pioneer ancestors."[65]

The Male Ideal

In addition to military service, men were most noted for Christianity, education, generosity, energy, and perseverance. Like their forebears of 1855, they were remembered for geniality, friendship, kindness, and devotion to family. However, a number of new attributes listed in 1870 *Times* obituaries were associated with business skills—efficiency, fidelity to the discharge of duty, accumulated wealth, command of language, industry, and attentiveness to work. One man was noted for his active membership in the chamber of commerce, another for the fact that he never indulged in risky financial speculation.[66]

Men's occupations listed in 1870 were more likely to be in the private sector than in 1855, including lawyer, flour and grain merchant, shipmaster, manufacturer of axes and scythes, railroad engineer, portrait painter, periodical editor, physician, hardware merchant, inventor, and member of the "Croton Aqueduct Department." Still, as in 1855, military officers and clergymen were also commemorated, as were public servants, including a mayor, superior court clerk, and congressman. Though most obituaries published in the *Times* in 1870 were still for upper- middle-class citizens, hints of class distinction began to creep into eulogies. Dr. Gunning Bedford, for example, was remembered for establishing the country's fist obstetrical clinic that

1855	New York Daily Times	New Orleans Picayune	Baltimore Sun
Men	Highly esteemed	Highly esteemed	Publicly esteemed
	Active	Amiable	Well-known
	Intelligent	Generous	Generous
	Scholarly	Intellectual	Honorable
	Manly	Educated	Having integrity
	Courteous	Gallant	Intellectual
	Strong of charcter	Talented	Noble
	Just	Manly	Industrious
	Honorable	Courteous	Wealthy
	Religious	True gentleman	Munificent
	Generous	Affectionate	Gallant
	Vigorous	Modest	Philanthropic
	Patriotic	Humorous	Heroic
	Gentle	Mannerly	Having democratic spirit
	Having integrity	Kind	Eminent
	Useful	Earnest	Prominent
	Honest	Useful	Respected
	Faithful	Brave	Distinguished
	Good husband/father	Energetic	Kind
	Humorous	Having integrity	Gentleman
		Having Ardor	Manly
		Respetable	Witty
		Excellent of character	Happy
			Unselfish
			Popular
			Devoted friend
			Competent
			Useful
			Having business capacity
Women	Christian	Christian	Christian
	Gentle	Good	Kind
	Kind	Having loving nature	Gentle
	Obliging	Amiable	Affectionate
	Honest	Kind	Modest
	Faithful	Gentle	Dutiful
	Beautiful	Pious	Sincere
	Talented	Relieving distress	Beloved wife
	Warm	Speaking noi ill	Devoted mother
	Happy	Patient	Meek
	Peaceful or calm in death	Resigned	Innocent
		Calm at death	Tender
		Affable	Mild
		Vivacious	Interesting
		Beautiful	Amiable
		Modest	Making home happy
		Intelligent	Well appearing

provided medical attention for "those who were too poor to pay a doctor's fee. It is estimated that over ten thousand poor people were annually visited."[67] And John McGrath was noted, in part, for organizing an Irish workingmen's association and for helping the city's "suffering poor."[68]

Women's Attributes

The few women eulogized in news obituaries in 1870 in the *New York Times* were noted for Christianity, fortitude in the face of death, sweet character, and usefulness, much like their 1855 forebears. However, social leadership and prominent position in fashionable society were mentioned in 1870, and Charlotte Lozier, a physician, not only earned an obituary in the news column but was eulogized three times. She was noted for her practice of medicine, her lectures, and her identification with the Women's Suffrage and Workingwomen's Associations. She was also remembered for her "genial, yet unassuming manner, her energy and perseverance as well as . . . her thorough womanliness and large-hearted generosity."[69] In a nation just ending a war for civil liberties, the *Times* made at least some small strides in including women in its news obituaries.

A Change in Emphasis

Not only was religious rhetoric and sentiment absent from *Times* obituaries in 1870, these notices were also far less likely to list specific causes of death than in 1855. Men and women were said to have died "suddenly" or of "lingering illnesses." One man, however, died from wounds received in a battle with pirates onboard a ship.[70] Other causes of death listed were cholera, inflammation or congestion of lungs, heart disease, apoplexy, inflammatory rheumatism, paralysis, consumption, typhus fever, pneumonia, kidney disease, dropsy of the brain, diphtheria and "acute disease."

As in 1855, the *Times* typically announced funeral arrangements in 1870 but was more likely to run descriptions of funerals of prominent citizens, listing dignitaries, crowds in attendance, and even flowers and coffins.[71] A preoccupation with wealth and status had also made its way into eulogies published five years after the Civil War.

New Orleans Picayune

Heroes of Commerce

Mark Walton

One by one the Old Guard of New Orleans merchants have passed away. Of all those who were engaged in commerce here sixty years ago but one remained—good, kind, noble old Mark Walton. Peters, Chow, Rolf, Planche, Lanfear, Gasquet, Zacharie and all the school of worthy old merchants passed away, and now Mark Walton has followed them—the last of his guild and class. He was a prominent merchant here when the ground on which the St. Charles Hotel, the City Hall and our office stand was a mere swamp. We believe he was a native of New Jersey and came to this city while a mere boy. He was still young when he participated as a volunteer in the great battle of the 8th January 1815. His life was one of continued devotion to business. He gathered property by his sagacity and energy, but was liberal to an extreme with his means and resources. He often lost heavily by his generous help to his mercantile confreres, but as often recovered by his indomitable will and industry. Had he been selfish he might have accumulated an enormous fortune. In spite of his generosity he made several fortunes. He was abstemious, regular and industrious in habits, an early riser, steady, thoughtful and methodical. He was noted for singular ability as an accountant and financier. He was eighty-five years of age, but retained his business habits to the last. New Orleans is noted for the amount of talent employed in commerce, but even to extreme age Mark Walton held his own with the ablest. He was noted for his skill as a bookkeeper and accountant and his books and papers are models of neatness, precision, method and order. Age rested kindly upon him without lessening his cheerfulness and buoyancy or detracting from his energy. Every step of his long and meritorious career was marked with generous deeds. He was honored and trusted by all his associates, noted always for fidelity and reliability.

Mark Walton leaves a son, the distinguished Col. J. B. Walton, and three daughters, Mrs. Martin, of New York, Mrs. Waldo and Miss Sarah Walton, of this city, besides a large number of grandchildren and great-grandchildren. They may all be proud of their pure, noble, worthy and generous ancestor.

New Orleans Picayune, 4 December 1870

Obituaries published in the *New Orleans Picayune* differed markedly from those in the *Times* in terms of patriotism. That quality, in fact, was not mentioned in *Picayune* obituaries published in 1870. The *Picayune*, however, raised preoccupation with wealth and status to a preeminent position. During the twelve weeks examined, the newspaper published 290 obituaries, 120 more than in 1855, including twenty-six news obituaries for men and one for a woman. Of the death notices, 51 percent were for men, 27 percent for women (only a slight increase from 1855), and 22 percent for children. Three Confederate soldiers were remembered in obituaries during these sample weeks. Charles Rufus Adams served in the First Confederate Company "until the surrender at Appomattox," but his obituary focused more on his fine capacity and great promise in business.[72] Colonel D. Beltzhoover served in the First Louisiana but also was eulogized for his devotion to the instruction of youth and his musical talents.[73] And Jules Oliver was noted for being a brilliant lawyer and "Creole gentleman of the highest class"—his courage in the war was mentioned simply at the end of the notice.[74]

Rather than war heroes, the *Picayune* was more likely to flatter successful businessmen in the 1870 obituary columns. Mark Walton, for example, was remembered for his devotion to business in making "several fortunes." This man "gathered property with sagacity and energy" and, at eighty-five, "retained his business habits to the last."[75] W. H. Chase was said to have lost much money in the war, but he retained "an ample fortune" and was remembered for his "courtly manner."[76] Wealth was the quality that earned seventy-three-year-old Lewis Ross, a prominent Cherokee, notice in a news obituary: "Being a merchant, he turned his whole attention to trade, and had but little to do with politics, and the Indians traveled far and near to trade with him. By that trade he acquired a very large fortune."[77] In 1870, wealth meant inclusion of a non-Caucasian on the obituary page. Indeed, acquisition of a large fortune was one of the most frequently mentioned attributes in *Picayune* obituaries in 1870, second only to deceased men who were true "gentlemen." Men were noted for attributes that would help them earn money, such as extraordinary enterprise in business, industry, bookkeeping skills, and business capacity, as well as for their gentlemanly qualities, including courtly manners, courtesy, goodness, honor, kindness, dignity, and hospitality. Men were also noted for Christianity and for being devoted husbands and fathers.

Men's occupations in the 1870 *Picayune* included newspaper editor, engineer, printer, infantry general, merchant, firefighter, district attorney, lawyer, circus manager, composer, actor, steamer pilot, proprietor of city gas works (Mobile), plantation owner, market commissioner, and doctor.

Status of Women

Women still bore illness with Christian fortitude and were gentle, amiable, and generous. Hannah Florence, however, had a "prepossessing appearance," had a "natural dignity of bearing," and was "frank, straightforward and truthful." She was noted for her charitable efforts after the war and for her class standing: "While courteous to equals, she was most kind to the lowly."[78] The *Picayune* eulogized Anna Cora Mowatt Ritchie, a well-known American author, although she resided in England.[79] Thus, just as in *The New York Times* during the same year, but unlike women in the Jacksonian era, a woman of 1870 in the could earn a news obituary in the *Picayune* based on her accomplishments rather than her relationship with men.

Causes of Death

Causes of death in the New Orleans newspaper, just as in the *Times*, were likely to be listed as a "long and painful illness" or "short illness." One man, however, was "shot by rowdies," another died fighting a fire, and another succumbed to "softening of the brain."[80] Among the few death causes listed were congestion of the brain, paralysis, dysentery, apoplexy, pneumonia, yellow fever, consumption, heart disease, and "disease of the vital organs." The *Picayune*, like the *Times*, described prominent citizens' lavish funerals, including a flowery description of the tomb and casket of Governor Henry Allen.[81] But like the *Times*, five years after the Civil War, the *Picayune* stopped using any kind of sentimental language in news obituaries (and little in the "Deaths" columns) about the passing of its citizens. Americans were indeed turning away from their preoccupation with death and focusing instead on commemorating the lives of the deceased.

Postwar Baltimore

The *Baltimore Sun* in 1870 published significantly more obituaries than it did in 1855, much like the *Times* and *Picayune*. The *Sun*'s 871 obituaries included sixty-eight in news columns, sixty (88 percent) for men and eight (12 percent) for women. Among those listed in the paid "Died" column, 34 percent were for men, 32 percent for women, and 34 percent for children.[82]

Service to both the Union and Confederacy played a prominent part in numerous 1870 *Sun* obituaries. For example, the front page of the 1 October edition contained a long account of the arrival of the remains of Admiral Farragut in New York, describing at length the military procession, coffin, and prominent assemblage at the funeral of the great admiral: "The remains were landed amid a thunderous salute of guns, and the funeral cortege, forming at once, proceeded on the march up Broadway in the face of a furious easterly storm."[83] Coleman Yellott, however, was remembered for leaving the Maryland Senate at the outbreak of war to eventually serve in the army of Virginia under General Robert E. Lee. He was "a firm supporter of what he believed to be the rights of the South," his obituary noted.[84] The war, just over, remained part of the national experience, and in this border town, soldiers on both sides of the conflict were commemorated in newspaper obituaries.

And in 1870, the *Sun* seemed to have held on to its proslavery sentiment. The obituary for Henry Black, a wealthy South Carolina planter, noted that he had owned five hundred slaves prior to the war and said he was "a model master in his relations towards them."[85] But the *Sun* also ran numerous accounts of the deaths of African Americans, although most contained some oddity that received more attention than did attributes of character. For example, an obituary with the headline "A Wealthy Colored Woman" said, "A colored woman, named Harriet Miller, died the other day in Philadelphia, leaving $100,000 worth of property. She was originally a slave in South Carolina, and derived her fortune from a rich planter named Purvis, who married her out of gratitude because she warned him of a conspiracy of his slaves against his life. After the death of Mr. Purvis she became the wife of Robert Miller a colored clergy. She was 85 years old."[86] This woman was newsworthy because of her fortune and her association with a wealthy planter and later a clergyman. Jane Loane, a black woman from Virginia, was commemorated because she died at the age of one hundred.[87] John Blake, described as "colored," was eulogized as a centenarian who had died at 103; his obituary also remarked that he was "well grown in the time of the revolutionary war, and remembered distinctly and frequently spoke of some of the officers who participated at the battle of Brandywine, at which he was present."[88] A. H. Galloway of Wilmington, North Carolina, was remembered in a short front-page obituary simply as a "colored State Senator and prominent republican politician."[89] It is difficult to determine how many African Americans were represented in the paid "Died" column: only one person was specifically identified as "colored."[90] News values may have paid a more distinct role than commemorative values in editors' decisions about publishing obituaries of African Americans, but these obituaries increasingly began appearing on the *Sun*'s pages in 1870.

The typical 1870 *Sun* obituary, however, was still for an upper-middle-class white citizen, just as in the *Times* and *Picayune*. As in 1855, male occupations listed included judge, doctor, minister, priest, state legislator, congressman, county clerk, professor, lawyer, printer, actor, dry goods merchant, police officer, newspaperman, hotel proprietor, author, wagoner, customs-house employee, mayor, naval officer, police commissioner, engineer, brewer, tobacconist, and dentist. Occupations for three women were listed—author, doctor, and actress.

The Baltimore Man

Being well-known, respected, eminent, and educated or learned were the male attributes most often listed. Knowledge about international affairs, literary ability, and knowledge of history and literature were specifically mentioned. And though wealth and status were factors in some of these commemorations, especially if the citizen made lavish donations to the city, these attributes were not as noteworthy as they were in the *Picayune* during the same sample weeks. A Baltimore man, it seemed, was more likely to be remembered for his genial disposition, gentle manners, ability to make friends, popularity, manners, generosity, and goodness. Many were beloved or held in esteem, and several were praised for being among the "Old Defenders of Baltimore" during the War of 1812.

The Loving Woman

Women, usually identified by their relationships to husbands or fathers, were described as loving, kind, respected, and beloved. Mary Dorsey, commemorated in a lengthy news obituary, was "extensively known and beloved." As her obituary noted: "This lady, who was distinguished for all the qualities which adorn her sex, left 51 direct descendants."[91] Two women identified with jobs were also given longer descriptions than other women during the sample weeks. Anna Cora Mowatt Ritchie, an author and actress, was remembered for her example and influence in elevating "the estimation in which the stage is held by society generally." Her obituary commemorated her worth as an individual, not just because of her association with a man, and noted, "No one today disputes the fact that a lady may emerge from private life into the glare of the footlights and be a lady still; but when Mrs. Mowatt went upon the stage this view of theatrical life had not been thoroughly adopted by the public at large." Though her work on the stage was admirable, this woman's obituary also pointed out that "her later years were adorned by all those domestic virtues which so long had also characterized her earlier life."[92] And in "The Death of a Well Known 'Doctress,'" a "Mrs. Dr. Lozier" was remembered for her extensive medical practice, which, according to her obituary, "sapped her strength at a time when she needed it most." Though the obituary seemed to criticize her devotion to her work, it also commemorated Lozier for other nontraditional attributes: "She was a lady of fine literary tastes, wrote frequently for the newspapers, and well known as a public speaker in the working women and woman suffrage movements."[93] Though the nation was half a century away from accepting women in the political franchise, the *Sun* in 1870 struggled with the notions of women in nontraditional roles, sending mixed signals about gender values for its Baltimore readers.

The Deaths

The *Sun* in 1870, like the *Times* and *Picayune*, dramatically decreased the listings of specific causes of death in both its paid and news obituaries. Unlike in 1855, most people died either suddenly or of short, protracted, or lingering illnesses. Specific causes mentioned included scarlet fever, consumption, pneumonia, brain congestion, heart disease, softening of the brain, drowning, being thrown from a horse, whooping cough, cholera, chronic croup, typhoid fever, railroad accidents, accidental shooting, dropsy, and liver congestion. And just as in the New York and New Orleans papers, news obituaries in the *Sun* included no sentimental verse or religious rhetoric. A few more verses ran in the *Sun*'s paid obituaries, but it was evident that either the paper provided examples or the deceased's families copied them. For example, one short poem was repeated numerous times, with the proper name inserted in the first line:

We had a little Nellie once;
She was our joy and pride;
We loved her, ah, perhaps too well;
For soon she slept and died.[94]

However, the somber deathbed scenes and lurid descriptions of the act of dying had disappeared from the *Sun*, like the *Picayune*, providing still more evidence of a society turning away from death.

Changes Reflected

Obituaries in the American press became more inclusive during the fifteen years surrounding the Civil War, although most people commemorated were still upper and middle class. More women were remembered, and business attributes gained in importance for men, as did qualities attainable by everyman, such as honesty, industry, generosity, energy, and kindness. However, in an era of new freedoms for African Americans, they were still virtually ignored unless they served some sort of news value. Obituary columns grew, true, but they were still likely primarily to include white men, providing evidence of a society struggling with ideas of inclusion and changing gender roles.

Regional differences were most apparent in men's obituaries following the Civil War: men in the *New York Times* were remembered for patriotism and gallant service in the war. Heroism, however, was reserved for the side of the victors, while southern men found solace in their gentlemanly virtues and ability to succeed in business despite the realities of Reconstruction. Men in the border city of Baltimore were remembered for their ability to get along with others—for being esteemed and kind and for having popular and gentle manners. If these obituaries are any indication, five years after the end of the Civil War, cultural regional differences were much stronger than they had been five years before it began.

Perhaps the most striking change from 1855 was the disappearance of sentimentality and religious rhetoric from obituaries in 1870. And all three newspapers seemed much more reluctant to mention a medical cause of death. It seems that five years after the end of the Civil War, people were weary of romanticizing the passing of their citizens. Exhausted from the horrors of war, Americans, then, began distancing themselves from the physical process of dying. Emerging medical science and funeral practitioners may have also eased this cultural change.

Characteristics in obituaries were also influenced by gender. In both eras, what was commemorated of a woman's life differed decidedly from what was deemed valuable in a man's—women generally were described in terms of their gentle, nurturing natures and relationships to men. Although more women were included in 1870 than in 1855, the vast majority still were remembered because of associations with men of prominence. However, after the war, each newspaper included obituaries of women because of their professions, indicating a small step toward the inclusion of women in the world outside the home, away from husbands or fathers. Evidence shows that these commemorations of the lives of individual citizens were intended to serve as examples to the public and to preserve those citizens' virtues for public memory. These death stories, indeed, reverberated throughout society and influenced the changing culture and national collective memory during this pivotal time in American history.

A NEW
CENTURY

Mrs. E. E. R. Peabody

Mrs. Eleanor E. R. Peabody, widow of Arthur J. Peabody, and one of the founders of the Colonial Dames of America, died yesterday at her home, 15 West Tenth Street. Her father, Archibald Russell, was the founder of the Five Points House of Industry, and her grandfather, the late Dr. John Watts, was the first President of the College of Physicians and Surgeons. Mrs. Peabody was a direct descendant of Gen. William Alexander, (Lord Stirling) a member of Gen. Washington's staff, and on her maternal side she was descended from Lewis Morris of Morrisania, signer of the Declaration of Independence.

Mrs. Peabody was a manager of the Home for the Destitute Blind and a Director of many of the parochial activities of Calvary Church.

New York Times, 5 November 1910

As the United States moved from the nineteenth century to the twentieth, the nation's social structures shifted, affecting the lives and the character of citizens. By the end of the 1920s Americans had changed spiritually, culturally, economically, and politically.[1] The new century indeed ushered in a more consumptive and less religious America, and with it came a dramatic, substantive change in the democracy. Seventy-two years after women gathered at Seneca Falls, New York, to hear radical calls for women's property rights and suffrage, ratification of the Nineteenth Amendment in 1920 finally affirmed woman's political franchise. Battles over who was worthy of full citizenship had become gender based, challenging long-held beliefs about women's role in the democracy and their duty to family.[2] Scholars differ in their interpretations of just how this new political role affected women in the decade following the amendment.[3] Did these changes affect average women or only a small group of those who were politically active? To provide one small piece of the puzzle, this chapter examines the newspaper obituaries published in mass-circulation newspapers before and after the 1920 ratification of the Nineteenth Amendment as reflectors of changing culture, gender inclusion in America, and public memory. Although women will be the primary focus here, men's obituaries of the era also offer clues about social inclusion.

This chapter incorporates all 4,163 obituaries of American citizens or residents published in the *New York Times*, *Chicago Tribune*, and *San Francisco Chronicle* during the first week of each month in 1910 and 1930. The San Francisco paper included in this chapter adds a new region, the West, where suffrage had been granted prior to 1920.

All three newspapers in these eras differentiated between an obituary and a paid death notice, with the latter giving only a chronicle of the death, funeral arrangements, and names of immediate family. Though far greater in number, these death notices were not commemorative in nature, so only obituaries are included here.

The Press

The *Times*, already a powerful force in New York, gained more prestige during World War I, and in the years following the paper increased its daily size from twenty-four pages to as many as forty and had a circulation near 500,000.[4] In Chicago, competition made the prosperous *Tribune* somewhat sensational, according to Frank Luther Mott, but the paper was well edited, "fairly conservative," in its political positions and successful enough to publish, by 1914, a seventy-two-page Sunday edition and erect a new $8 million building in 1924–25.[5] In the West, the *San Francisco Chronicle* had used crusades and community projects to make a name for itself as the great San Francisco paper of the late nineteenth century, maintaining a strong circulation well into the twentieth century. Unlike its competition, the successful Hearst-owned *Examiner*, with its operations based in New York, control of the *Chronicle* remained in the region.[6] Obituaries published in each of these papers provide contrasting insight into publicly stated cultural values and public memory in these eastern, midwestern, and western regions during this crucial time in American history.

Just as America was changing at the turn of the century, so too was the press, and these changes likely had an impact on obituary coverage. The newspaper was still the powerhouse of the American media,[7] and mainstream papers, dependent on high circulations and advertising revenue, promoted a consumer culture and looked for ways to attract new audiences. Journalists, while developing ideals of professionalism, objectivity, and public service, also made celebrities of entertainers and gangsters and practiced tabloid-style sensationalism.[8] This was the era of the crusading muckrakers, who investigated and prompted reform of social ills, but it was also the era of "yellow journalists" who exaggerated news, perpetrated hoaxes, and fabricated interviews.[9] The power of newspapers and such journalistic paradoxes concerning content likely affected obituary inclusion.

Lessons for Obituary Writers

As journalism moved toward professionalization, specialization, and even sensationalism, handbooks on newswriting became available, giving tips for working journalists and would-be reporters. These texts promoted specific writing styles and encouraged the use of uniform sources. As an established part of news content, obituaries were discussed as potential human-interest features. But the handbooks also reflect standardization in content during this period. For example, in 1911 Charles Ross in *The Writing of News* gave tips to reporters on gathering specific kinds of information for obituaries, and then he gave advice on the style and tone of an obituary: "Let your story be simple and dignified, in keeping with the theme."[10]

By 1925 the growing funeral industry had a hand in influencing obituary content.[11] In *Getting the News*, William S. Maulsby instructed reporters to "talk to every undertaker in the city every day" for the death notices. The undertakers would be cooperative, he assured, because having their names in obituaries was good for business. "In writing ordinary obituary notices, it is best to follow a strict, stereotyped form," he wrote. But Maulsby was quick to note that reporters should "act on the theory that any man has had at least one interesting thing happen to him" and that a "prominent man" deserved still more attention, including interviews with colleagues, descriptions of his career, and even the size of his estate. Reporters, he advised, could learn about a man's prominence by "his place of residence" or even by paying attention to "the names of some of the persons who sent flowers for the funeral." Obituary writers were to be careful with the facts: "Inaccuracies in obituaries are unpardonable." And writers were to be considerate of readers: "When death is due to a common disease, the cause is not ordinarily mentioned in consideration for the feelings of readers of the paper who may be suffering from the same disease," he cautioned.[12] Maulsby's instructions indicate an agenda of promoting prominence as a noteworthy attribute in a newspaper obituary.

Death news soon became a way to increase circulation. One 1935 reporting guide wrote, "News of the death of well known person is always certain to interest thousands of readers. . . . The bigger the renown of the dead person, the bigger the appeal of the story. . . . The more sudden and unexpected the death, the better the story."[13] In *A College Course in Reporting for Beginners*, Curtis D. MacDougall gave specific guidelines for making obituaries as standardized as possible, including five elements for the lead, six for the body of the story, and even an "obituary blank," a printed form for undertakers who cooperated in providing information. He did, however, offer the reporter some leeway for "side features," including anecdotes, outstanding career events, and even "first-person reminiscences" of individuals close to the deceased.[14] Obituaries of the era, then, were influenced by press concerns over circulation and by funeral directors, but evidence in these texts shows that the deceased's family, friends, and business associates still had at least some input into obituary content.

A Cultural Shift

Because of the dramatic cultural changes Americans experienced at the turn of the century, and because of the evolutions in press conventions, obituaries in both 1910 and 1930 differed significantly from nineteenth-century obituaries. For example, one major difference was in the area of religious imagery, so prominent in obituaries of the Jacksonian and Civil War eras. A Puritan ethic had dominated the spiritual and moral thinking of nineteenth-century Americans, but more modern Americans had different ideas about religion. With the dawn of the new century, Protestant culture had become less rigid, with fewer rules.[15] Because, as Joseph A. Amato wrote, death stories reverberate with religion and culture,[16] newspaper obituaries, a recognized forum for relating death stories, provide some evidence of the changing spiritual beliefs and religious uncertainty in early-twentieth-century America. However, press ideals of professionalism temper that evidence.

Economically, America had become a society of consumers.[17] The small business run by the sober, virtuous man of will of the early and mid–nineteenth century gave way to the large, bureaucratic corporation of the twentieth. This new economy wrested away the average working man's autonomy: work became increasingly specialized and city-centered. Decisions citizens had always made individually, and tasks they had always performed independently, were now controlled by others. T. J. Jackson Lears argues that this phenomenon only strengthened American feelings of weightlessness and unreality.[18]

Warren Susman writes about the turn-of-the century shift from a character-based culture to a personality-based culture.[19] A strong will might have been necessary for the entrepreneur of the nineteenth century, but only a man who could get along with corporate bosses and colleagues could survive in the twentieth. Newspaper obituaries, especially those for men, who still dominated the workforce, commemorate virtues that were more oriented to personality than to character, to business rather than to home.

Gender Roles

But what about women? Perhaps the most startling change in the early twentieth century was that of American attitudes about gender. No longer was woman the moral guardian of the home as she had been in the Victorian era. With the industrial age and the suffrage movement, women in the 1920s embraced new ideas about their public behavior and began breaking down barriers of discrimination.[20] But as Lears points out, changes in the economy gave women new socially prescribed functions, but they were still domestic roles. In the early twentieth century, he argues, women became the target of advertisers who described their products as deliverers not only of an ordered life but also of "authentic experience."[21] Gender roles shifted, but the vast majority of men and women followed the social rules of the new industrial economy by maintaining order and the power structure. Obituaries in this era, especially those for women, reflected these new gender roles as well as expectations of the dominant culture.

Politically, however, women had for the first time a constitutional invitation into the world of politics, or at least into the voting booth. Mary Fainsod Katzenstein points to the "outbreak of new organizational activities by women," including social reform and pacifist groups, numerous professional associations, and political organizations, as evidence of women working to gain full citizenship: "In the 1920s, women demonstrated what they had learned from the century-long struggle for suffrage . . . that they had the right to act as public persons—to be active in the open spaces of political life . . . in all spheres of society and politics."[22] Obituaries published before and after the 1920 ratification of the Nineteenth Amendment reflect changing ideas about women as citizens, both as voters and as public persons.

The Woman of 1910
The New York Times
Wealth and Status

FRANCES A. SCHARFF, widow of Christian H. Scharff, and the niece of William H. Seward, Secretary of State under President Lincoln, died at the home of her brother, Dr. F. W. Seward at Goshen, N.Y., yesterday. She was 74 years old.
New York Times, 7 February 1910

KATHERINE HYDE RAY HURLBUT, widow of Samuel Hurlbut of Baltimore and Connecticut and daughter of the late Surgeon Hyde Ray of the United States Navy, is dead at her residence, 194 Clinton Street, Brooklyn. She is survived by her two sons, Samuel Ray and Wilson M. Hurlbut. Funeral Services will be held at St. Anne's Protestant Episcopal Church, Annapolis, Md.
New York Times, 7 December 1910

In fact, women's lives were not greatly commemorated in 1910. Women represented only 15 percent of the 1,059 *New York Times* obituaries published during the sample weeks. Thus, while women were considered more newsworthy in the *Times* than they had been in 1870, when only 10 percent received news obituaries, a smaller percentage of women was commemorated in 1910. Death notices for women in 1870, 40 percent of the total, often included commemorative information, but these paid death notices in the *Times* in 1910 included only facts about the death and the funeral and did not list attributes.

Obituaries in 1910, then, reflected a culture that valued men, money, and industry. In the first category, name and occupation of the deceased, most women were identified by associations with husbands, fathers, brothers, or sons. These women's obituaries commemorated the deceased less for their personal attributes than for their husbands' business accomplishments. The obituary for Elizabeth Schack, for example, remembered her as the widow of Otto Wilhelm Christian Schack, former secretary of the New York Stock Exchange, and for being the daughter-in-law of a member of a private stock-exchange firm.[23] Several obituaries described occupations and accomplishments of fathers, sons, grandfathers, sons-in-law, and even more distant relations. The lead paragraph of one piece, for example, said, "Mrs Albert E. Plant, whose husband is the first cousin of the late Henry B. Plant, the railroad and steamship owner, was killed this morning by the express train for New York City."[24] In an industrial society that valued profit and production, these women's lives were greatly overshadowed by the lives of men who represented those attributes.

Obituaries of the era, however, do offer evidence of a society struggling with changing ideas about a woman's place. A few women were remembered for roles they played outside the home, particularly social roles. Edith Walsh Marshall, for example, was "one of the most popular of the younger society women of Greenwich and a member of several organizations."[25] And Boston native Mrs. Pierre L. Ronalds, who died in Paris, was "well known in many European Courts, first for her beauty and later for her social talents for almost half a century."[26] These women were commemorated not for domestic virtue but for social prominence, personality, or beauty that likely helped husbands, at least indirectly, succeed in business.

Unlike nineteenth-century obituaries and death notices, *Times* obituaries in 1910 did not describe the deceased women as gentle, kind, obliging, honest, or faithful. In fact, the articles seldom listed character traits at all. Rather, in describing attributes of the deceased, these obituaries promoted what appeared to be the period's socially accepted value of a woman's life. Many women were described as "well-known" or "prominent," indicating a social station. Adelaide Tukey was not a wealthy woman, but her obituary still illustrates the importance of social prominence: she was described as "the long-familiar figure of the 'Little Old Lady of the Cashmere Shawl'" who "was small of figure and habitually wore a fine cashmere shawl, which many persons sought to buy from her at a high price, but, with which she would never part." As her obituary noted, "she was well known to everyone . . . and was warmly welcomed in the homes of even the most exclusive families."[27] Such invitations merited Miss Tukey notice on the *Times* obituary page.

In addition to social prominence, wealth was an important attribute for women in *Times* obituaries, which even occasionally listed the size of women's estates. Sometimes a widow struggled when left without enough money to survive, and two obituaries recalled the lives of women who overcame difficult financial times to support themselves. Flora Darling's wealth "was lost in unprofitable investments, but she retrieved, to some extent, her losses through the sale of her books."[28] Eliza Haverly's husband had made considerable money performing in minstrel shows but left little of it: "His widow has supported herself by selling cold cream and cosmetics in a small West Forty-Second Street Office," her obituary noted.[29] A stash of money was enough to warrant a *Times* obituary even for an eccentric hermit. Emily Williams "was 70 years old and had been known locally as Old Maid Williams. . . . She was reputed to have wealth to the extent of about $40,000. One of her habits was to carry concealed about her person a package of bankbooks, but these books have not been found though searched for."[30] Even though Miss Williams lacked the all-important association with a husband, her $40,000 interested the *Times*. Wealth was indeed a noteworthy virtue in 1910.

Contributions Remembered

Miss CLARA A. KNOWLES, who was for twenty-eight years the Superintendent of the Wayside Home in Bridge Street, Brooklyn, died there on Saturday night. Credit was given Miss Knowles for the reformation of many young women who had been sent to the institution from the police courts. The body was taken to Centreport, Me., for burial.

New York Times, 1 November 1910

A few women of the era were remembered for contributions that had little to do with wealth or status. Several women mentioned in the *Times* were educators, including teachers and a principal; some were nurses; and others were well-known as authors. Emily Briggs, for example, gained fame as a newspaper correspondent and author of the "Olivia Letters" during the Civil War.[31] Myra Kelly was known for the "pathos and humor" in her books about the lives of immigrant children. The author "endeared herself to thousands of readers" and had received a letter from Theodore Roosevelt, who was "deeply impressed with the true ring" of her stories.[32] Women were also involved in social work and in significant religious work—obituaries appeared for missionaries, the chaplain of the Young Women's Christian Association, a preacher in the Society of Friends, a Methodist Episcopal deaconess, and, in one of the most extensive obituaries of 1910, the founder of the Christian Scientists, Mary Baker Eddy. Her front-page obituary, illustrated with two photographs and a ten-deck headline, discussed the secrecy surrounding her death, the estimated size of her estate at $1 million, the question of her successor, and her requests for a simple funeral. The article also included news interviews with some of her admirers, who remembered her "many charitable and public-spirited acts" and noted her as "the leader of a religious movement which has deeply impressed itself on the world."[33] Other women represented included an actress, a hotel proprietor, a real estate operator, and a seamstress in an underwear factory, but most of the employed women in 1910 worked in traditional nurturing roles associated with education, nursing, literature, and religion.

Ten years before ratification of the Nineteenth Amendment, only two women were remembered in the *Times* for any kind of political role. Anna M. Hammer "was widely known for her intense interest in philanthropic and temperance work. Of 'Revolutionary Quaker stock,' she was for years prominently identified with the work of the Women's Christian Temperance Union."[34] And Augusta Cooper Bristol, a "prominent figure" on the lecture platform, "made the address nominating Gen. Benjamin F. Butler for President of the United States on the Greenback ticket, and delivered the principal address before the Women's Conference of the World's Fair at Chicago."[35] Although Hammer's obituary listed her husband's name and the occupations of her father, grandfather, and uncle, the commemoration of Mrs. Bristol's life included only her own accomplishments. Sparse in number, these *Times* obituaries offer evidence of a society struggling with, though not necessarily opposed to, a woman's voice in politics at a time when women did not have the right to vote.

Regional Differences

Criteria for Inclusion

Although there were a few regional differences, obituaries for women in the *Chicago Tribune* and *San Francisco Chronicle* during sample weeks in 1910 resembled those in the *Times* in percentages as well as in content. In the *Tribune*, 18 percent of the 317 obituaries were for women, as were 18 percent of the 134 obituaries in the *Chronicle*, a slightly higher rate than the *Times*'s 15 percent. Some of the same women were commemorated in all three papers, indicating that their obituaries received national attention, including authors, actresses, and Eddy, who received long obituaries in both the *Tribune* and the *Chronicle* and even was featured in a special supplement in the *Tribune*.[36] As one of the *Chronicle* articles noted, she "opened that little boarding house and called it the 'Massachusetts Metaphysical College.' It is said of her that she had no idea in the earlier days of that college that great riches would be poured into her lap, that there would be wholesale desertions from other and older congregations."[37] Though Eddy's obituary treatment was not typical of other women in 1910, the exemplars mentioned and the anecdotes used reflected spiritual leadership and the value of great wealth.

Just as in the *Times*, the attributes most often listed for women were associations with men. Women's obituaries in both the *Tribune* and the *Chronicle* often gave lengthy descriptions not of their accomplishments or character but of their husbands' careers. Many obituaries mentioned social prominence and popularity. The few occupations named were educator, author, and religious or social worker.

The Pioneer Woman

Rather than list traits of character, the *Tribune* and *Chronicle*, like the *Times*, described what was considered worthy of remembering about a 1910 woman's life. And the western newspapers featured a different ideal, the pioneer. In San Francisco, obituaries for female pioneers included descriptions of the route they took to reach the West. Many were first-generation pioneer women, such as Mrs. J. Rasmussen, who came from Germany, and Mrs. A. F. Ladd, who arrived in 1853 from Quebec.[38] Others were not first-generation Americans, like Mrs. C. M. Haun, described as the "widow of [a] prominent pioneer," born in Kentucky, and married at nineteen and who "crossed the plains in 1849."[39] Pioneer Abigail B. Hunt, who had lived in California for fifty-four of her one hundred years, was commemorated for her longevity and robust health, which was "excellent up to several weeks before she died."[40] The *Tribune* obituaries, though less likely to call a woman a "pioneer," focused on where women were born and their routes to Chicago. Ireland and Germany were the foreign origins of birth most often mentioned. Two women, however, were remembered for being among the first white children born in their American communities.[41] And, because of previous publicity in the *Tribune*, Dinah E. Munger Sprague was able to create an image of pioneer nostalgia with her own words. As her obituary said, "About three years ago she granted a reporter an interview and said: 'My father felled the first tree and planted the first potato in west central New York. We wore homespun clothes, and on Sunday went to church in an ox cart.'" Noted for her longevity, Sprague's "ambition to pass the century mark" symbolized a nostalgia for the pioneer days and admiration for long life and robust health, all strong factors in these women's obituaries in 1910.[42]

Women's obituaries also linked them with events and symbols of America's past, elements of public memory that scholars say bind a society together.[43] The most obvious reference was membership in the Daughters of the American Revolution, a society for women who could trace their ancestry back to revolutionary days. In fact, Flora

Adams Darling, who founded the organization and was the widow of a Confederate soldier in the Civil War, was among the women commemorated in the *Tribune* in 1910.[44] Lovina Streight, known as the "northern angel" during the Civil War, served as a Union spy in Confederate hospitals.[45] Sprague was remembered not only for being a "pioneer woman" in Chicago but also for being the granddaughter of an officer in George Washington's army; her obituary thus commemorated, through a patriotic symbol, her memory as well as her family's generational memory.[46] And her obituary shows Washington's lingering strength as an icon in American public memory.

Twentieth-Century Men
Inclusion

MINNEAPOLIS, May 8—Levi M. Stewart, said to be the richest man in Minneapolis, died today of inflammation of the lungs. He held more real estate in Minneapolis than any other man, and his estate is computed to be worth many millions. For many years he lived the life of an eccentric bachelor in a small wooden shanty situated in the heart of the city.

New York Times, 4 May 1910

ROBERT H. SHEARER, one of the wealthiest and best known merchants in the Mohawk Valley, died at his home in Fort Plain, N.Y., yesterday at the age of 82. For many years he was Director of Fort Plain National Bank, and had been President of the institution for the last ten years. He left $250,000.

New York Times, 3 February 1910

What about the occupations and attributes of men who died in 1910? Obituaries in all three newspapers offered stark gender contrast. In the *New York Times*, 85 percent of the obituaries published in the sample weeks were for men, commemorated for their hard work, wealth, power, education, and memberships in male associations and fraternal organizations. In fact, the attribute most often listed for men in *Times* obituaries in 1910 was the number of years worked.

The *Times* in 1910 listed hundreds of men's occupations, though most men commemorated were upper-middle to upper class in professional, educational, or economic status. Many were described as company founders, bank presidents, industrialists or manufacturers, wealthy merchants, brokers, or powerful political figures, such as judges or former senators or congressmen. Several were labeled "capitalists." These men were often associated with not simply one corporation but with many simultaneously. Others were bureaucrats or had jobs that represented a workforce increasingly specialized, including, for example, municipal or court clerks, city controllers, bailiffs, tax commissioners, the New York Telephone Company division equipment superintendent, and the Brooklyn superintendent of steamrollers. Some obituaries reflected the national interest in sports, remembering athletes, a racehorse trainer, a yacht master, and a football coach. Reminiscent of obituaries from the nineteenth century, occupations included numerous clergymen, educators, physicians, journalists, and public servants, representing a society and a press that still valued those roles. Unlike in the nineteenth century, however, only a smattering of military officers were included in 1910, though prior service in the Civil War was mentioned. Obituaries for men with less prominent occupations were included if the person represented another value, such as longevity. For example, railroad baggage man Michael O'Rourke was remembered for being the oldest in his occupation.[47]

Male Attributes

Attributes highlighted for deceased men differed significantly from those nineteenth-century obituaries, just as the women's attributes did. In 1910 character traits were seldom mentioned but were implied based on long lists of professional accomplishments and associations. For example, the work ethic was valued: a large number of obituaries described men who had spent ten to fifty years in the same profession, even with the same company. Many men were retired, but their obituaries often assured readers that they labored right up until their health failed. Eighty-two-year-old Joshua Crosby, for example, who had been employed at the customshouse since the Civil War, remained at work until the Saturday night before he died.[48] Professor Samuel S. Sanford, "worth several million dollars," worked "from sheer enjoyment."[49] And William H. Class "worked for forty-five years without a break in the Manhattan Building Department."[50] One obituary, which eulogized the late president of the Chamber of Commerce as well as "other great leaders," reminded readers "of the quick passing of a generation of business men who have wrought mightily for the building up of this continent."[51] Thus, *Times* male obituaries of 1910 reflected a society that expected men to value work and to be loyal to the corporation. This America credited businessmen for building the nation, a patriotic value.

Other oft-mentioned attributes about men's lives in the 1910 *Times* were their college or university affiliations and their origins in countries including Germany, Ireland, England, Romania, and Holland. A few men were described as "unmarried," though most were said to be survived by a widow and children. Descriptors most often used for men were "well-known," "widely known," or "best-known," "prominent," "authority," "wealthy," "oldest," and "millionaire." The descriptors "capitalist" and "philanthropist" were used; numerous obituaries listed real estate holdings or dollar amounts of the estates of the deceased,[52] with some guessing if the exact amount was not known. For example, the obituary for John S. Huyler, described as a millionaire candy manufacturer, said, "Just how wealthy Mr. Huyler was nobody seems to know exactly. His estate is probably worth many millions, perhaps ten, perhaps twenty."[53] In addition to a work ethic and company loyalty, men's obituaries the *Times* in 1910 offer evidence that money and prominence were important social ideals.

Obituaries for men in the 1910 *Chicago Tribune* and *San Francisco Chronicle* also emphasized long years of work, immense wealth, and social prominence. Men commemorated in both newspapers had jobs similar to those in the *Times*, reflecting an industrial society increasingly specialized and bureaucratic; these men also were members of numerous associations, including professional organizations, civic clubs, athletic clubs, ethnic clubs, and lodges.

Pioneer Spirit

Just as in the women's obituaries of 1910, the *Tribune* and *Chronicle* tended to value the deceased men's pioneer origins. In fact, in the *Chronicle*, the descriptor "pioneer" was used repeatedly in men's obituaries, including pioneer residents, a pioneer clothier, pioneer harness maker, and pioneer banker.[54] The *Chronicle* painted a nostalgic picture of those pioneer days. For example, the obituary for a former sheriff said, "Thrilling stories of the days when desperadoes held full sway in the section of California included in Monterey and San Benito counties are being recalled with the news of the death . . . late yesterday afternoon of Thomas Watson."[55] Daniel Luce, who "crossed the plains" in 1846, lived in the days when there was no ferry service or army boats to San Francisco. His obituary noted, "Luce built one of the first rowboats on the bay in order to visit the future metropolis of the coast."[56] The *Tribune* remembered Henry Aldrich as the "first white male child born in Henry County, Illinois." He was "for years known to the Indians of the vicinity by the name of 'White Papoose' and retained to his death many presents from savages."[57] Melville Weston Fuller, a chief justice of the U.S. Supreme Court, was also commemorated in the *Tribune* for living up to the pioneer spirit of his ancestors. His obituary recalled that he "sprang from sturdy New England pioneers, men who had fought the battles against the wilderness and had conquered, who had fought their own way to prominence and had succeeded."[58] Obituaries in these western newspapers not only recognized wealth and prominence but honored the spirit of the white settler and conqueror.

The *Tribune* and *Chronicle* were both more likely to include sensationalism, even hints of scandal, in their obituaries, although these occasions were rare. The *Tribune*, for example, recounted former Senator T. C. Platt's "domestic troubles," including allegations of infidelity.[59] H. B. Lindley's death was attributed to his morphine habit, with the headline "Brilliant, but Errs; Dies." Once a successful lawyer and author, Lindley himself gave the account of his demise in a statement to the *Tribune* that told of the sad and bitter "years of downfall." As his obituary stated, Lindley died "in abject poverty, shunning relatives and friends of his prosperous days, with faculties impaired by years of dissipation."[60] In these years of muckrakers and yellow journalists, an obituary not only commemorated the ideal in society but was an example of unworthiness, how not to live. Obituaries might include character traits both good and bad, the ideal as well as the negative model.

Historic Symbols

SAW LINCOLN SLAIN; IS DEAD

Educator of the Deaf and Dumb Who Was Present in the Theater at Assassination Succumbs

Indianapolis, Inc., Jan 3.—Prof. W. H. Demotte, for sixty years one of the most prominent educators of the deaf and dumb in the United States, died early today at his home in this city. He was 80 years old, and was born at Harrodsburg, Ky.

He went to Washington as Indiana military agent during the civil war, and was in Ford's theater the night president Lincoln was assassinated.

Prof. Demotte did not often describe the scene in words, but he vividly reproduced it in the sign language and pantomime for his students.

Chicago Tribune, 4 January 1910

Men's obituaries in all three newspapers in 1910, like those for women, provide evidence of a relationship between those obituaries and American public memory of a valued past. In addition to the pioneer references, obituaries linked the deceased with other valued historical events and symbols such as the American Revolution; the Forty-Niners, men who went West across the plains in 1849 looking for gold; and President Abraham Lincoln. In the *Chronicle*, for example, D. C. Breed was remembered for being a descendent of a revolutionary family, and Drury James was recalled as "one of the heroes who dated their entrance into California in the classic year of '49."[61] The *Tribune* commemorated another of the "boys of '49," along with men with some link to Abraham Lincoln: John Henderson was remembered for being a member of the mounted company that guarded Lincoln during the war, and Professor W. H. Demotte was recognized for being in Ford's Theater the night the president was assassinated.[62] In fact, an association with a patriotic symbol in American public memory was the only attribute that warranted the obvious inclusion of African Americans on the obituary pages in 1910. Moses Webb was described in his *Tribune* obituary as "an old negro who is said to have been the last survivor of the eight 'contrabands' who led the horses attached to the hearse at the funeral of Abraham Lincoln. . . . Webb was born a slave in 1825."[63] The *Times* remembered Gordon Davis for having been born a slave to Jefferson Davis and later for serving in the Union army.[64] Participation in a shared American experience and a relationship with the symbols of America's public memory were indeed a strong part in the socially accepted notion of what was valuable about these Americans' lives.

Causes of Death and Funerals

PIONEER CHICAGO SHOWMAN IS DEAD

George A. Fair Suddenly Expires at Norwood Park Residence.

PROMOTED COMIC OPERA.

Wedded Star of an Early Local Theater and Was a Great-Grandfather at 54

George A. Fair, pioneer theatrical manager and promoter of Chicago, died suddenly early yesterday at his Norwood Park residence of heart failure. He was 56 years old.

His last hours were dramatic. Mr. Fair had been troubled for a few weeks with what physicians diagnosed as indigestion. Some member of his family awaited at the depot his return nightly from Chicago.

Mr. Fair was accompanied Wednesday evening by Frank M. Buck, with whom he was associated. At the station J. H. Miers, his grandson, met Mr. Fair.

As the veteran and his grandson neared the residence, Mr. Fair, without uttering a word, fell into the young man's arms. In his room he was attacked with a coughing spell and swooned again, striking a trunk as he fell. A few minutes later he died.

Weds After Love at First Sight

Mr. Fair came to Chicago in 1866 as employe of the Crosby Opera house. Six years later he became advance agent of the Sawtelle Dramatic company, of which Miss Melissa Breslau was the star. He married her after a "love at first sight" romance at the age of 19.

Mr. Fair was connected with the advertising department of THE TRIBUNE for nine years and later engaged in other advertising work.

Mr. Fair was the only Chicago theatrical man who repeatedly "came back" after failure. He died "in harness"—as promoter of the Policeman's Benevolent association vaudeville which closes tomorrow at Orchestra hall. He induced the policemen to present their first benefit play in 1887, and this year, when they were about to abandon the idea for lack of a production and theater he hit upon the vaudeville idea.

He was born in Ipswich, England. He was associated with Will J. Davis in the old Columbia theater and later managed the Haymarket theater.

Promoted Comic Opera.

He added to the popularity of comic opera with ballets and other spectacular ideas in those days.

Mr. Fair attracted attention two years ago when at the age of 54 he became a great-grandfather. He was a father at 19 and a grandfather at 38.

The body will lie at an undertaking establishment at 3118 Irving Park boulevard until Sunday, when funeral services will be held in the chapel at 2 o'clock. Garden City Lodge No. 11 will be in charge. Interment will be at Montrose.

Chicago Tribune, 7 October 1910

What can the remaining two categories of obituary information, cause of death and funeral arrangements, reveal about Americans in 1910? Many obituaries now included specific causes of death. Some were quite different than those recorded in 1800s obituaries. In the new industrial age, for example, many people died in automobile accidents. In fact, in the *Times*'s sample examined, seven men died in auto-related accidents, most of them "struck down" by cars. But in this era when work, wealth, and social prominence remained all-important, the most common cause of death mentioned for both men and women was by far heart disease. Unlike other fairly common causes of death such as pneumonia, meningitis, and stomach disorders, obituaries detailed closely sudden heart attacks. People "dropped dead while plowing" or "died suddenly . . . of heart disease while sitting in a chair."[65] Clarence McIlhenney "dropped dead while waltzing on the White Star liner Adriatic," and his obituary provided a graphic description of him as he "staggered toward the rail of the sea deck . . . and collapsed."[66] In the *Tribune*, theatrical promoter George Fair's "last hours were dramatic. . . . In his room he was attacked with a coughing spell and swooned again, striking a trunk as he fell. A few minutes later he died."[67] Another social anxiety about medicine and death was common, as found in 1910 obituaries. Numerous people died "following an operation" rather than from a specific disease. The headline regarding the death of former Florida governor Napoleon Broward, for example, said that he died "under knife."[68] Daniel Luce, one of the pioneers in the *Chronicle*, "had never known a sick day" before an arm operation, from which he "failed to rally."[69] The deck and photograph caption concerning the death of capitalist Frederick Zeile referred to his operation.[70]

Another interesting change in the cause of death category was the introduction, though rare, of suicide as the mentioned cause of death. In prior sample years examined for this study, suicides were treated strictly as news stories and excluded from the obituary columns. But in 1910, that rule had begun to relax. For example, Edwin H. Terrell, a former minister to Belgium, shot himself in a "fit of melancholia" but was remembered on the obituary page for his "considerable important work in various capacities for the United States government."[71] Annie Ruppert hanged herself but was remembered for being the mother of a five-month-old child.[72] Cause of death in obituaries in 1910 reflect social anxieties about heart attacks, possibly the ramification of a society obsessed with work and wealth, anxieties about medical science, and the relaxing of a social taboo against acknowledging suicide.

Apart from the descriptions of sudden deaths, the powerful death imagery and religious rhetoric that were so important in nineteenth-century obituaries were not a part of obituaries in the 1910 sample weeks, likely because of changing ideas about religion and the press's increasing professionalism. But certain words and catchphrases appeared repeatedly in both headlines and articles. Unlike the Jacksonians, who endured nineteenth-century disease with Christian patience and met death without a murmur, people in 1910 "succumbed" to death or were "called" by death with no religious imagery or promise in their obituaries. Many obituaries, however, reassured readers that at the time of death the deceased was surrounded by family members, sometimes summoned quickly by telegraph. John G. Carlisle, a lawyer and former cabinet officer, was said to murmur parting words to those at his bedside: "He realized that the end was near, and whispered good-bye to all."[73] Citizens who died in 1910 concentrated on the parting, on family good-byes, rather than on the promise of Christian resurrection or a visitation from the "King of Terrors."

The vast majority of obituaries were published prior to funerals and listed only information about the time, date, and place of services. However, there were some descriptions of funerals, particularly for actors, celebrities, or clergy.[74] These obituaries referred to the large numbers of people in attendance, though the articles often pointed out that the deceased had requested a simple service. Again, funeral services reflected a paradox of values, emphasizing pomp and ceremony but not quite ready to give up the egalitarian ideal of simplicity.

Death after Suffrage

Women

Mrs. Christine Ladd-Franklin, Educator, Dies

Helped Open University Doors to Women

New York, March 5—(AP)—Mrs. Christine Ladd-Franklin, noted educator, logician and psychologist, and wife of Dr. Fabian Franklin, author, editor and mathematician, died today at her home in Riverside Drive. She was 82 years old.

Mrs. Franklin was born at Windsor, Conn. She was graduated from Vassar in 1860. Her career did much to open higher education to women. She was one of the first women admitted to study in Johns Hopkins university taking special examinations given by her future husband in order to work for the degree of Doctor of Philosophy.

Johns Hopkins Lecturer

Once in the Johns Hopkins, her ability was recognized by the award of fellowships for three successive years, and she served there as a lecturer from 1904 to 1909. Her degree, however, was not awarded until 1926, although she had completed her work for it on schedule.

After her marriage to Dr. Franklin, she accompanied her husband to Germany for study, but because of her sex was unable to gain admission to Professor G. E. Muller's courses at Goettingen. Muller, however, repeated his lecture course for her in his private laboratory, and permitted her to work there.

HAD INFLUENCE IN BERLIN

Later, on Prof. Muller's recommendation, she was admitted to the Prussian Kultusminister at Berlin. Her study there and in other Berlin laboratories was credited with being the opening wedge for women's studying in German universities. She had been a lecturer at Columbia University since 1910.

She is survived by her widower and a daughter, Margaret Franklin, author of "The Case for Woman Suffrage."

Chicago Tribune, 6 March 1930

Twenty years later, a decade after the Nineteenth Amendment guaranteed women a place in the political process, the *New York Times*'s 1,923 obituaries still included only 18 percent women. But while the numbers of women commemorated had increased by just 3 percent from 1910, the substance had changed significantly.

Though many women still were remembered only by their husbands' business occupations, more and more working women were represented on the obituary page. The jobs listed for women still included the familiar educator, author, actor, artist, or writer, but now the obituaries noted more nontraditional occupations, some that indicated economic and political power. Highlighted in the 1930 *Times* were Mary L. Keating, a retired racehorse trainer, Julia C. Montague, owner of a confectionary manufacturing company, and E. Alberta Read, assistant chief of the microanalytical laboratory of the Department of Agriculture's Bureau of Chemistry.[75] Mrs. Robert Rankin was acknowledged as an expert on the causes of war and advised, in her publications, ways to make the League of Nations more effective.[76] One of the lengthiest *Times* obituaries in 1930 recalled contributions of Mary "Mother" Jones, "militant crusader for the rights of the laboring man."[77] Even in the more familiar occupations, women wielded more influence. Rather than being a teacher or principal, for example, Sister Mary Bernard was supervisor of parochial schools in her community; rather than being an army nurse, Dr. Elizabeth L. Peck ran the West Philadelphia Hospital for Women.[78] Agnes Randolph, called a leading woman executive and the founder of an outpatient tuberculosis service in Virginia, was credited in her obituary with cutting in half the state's rates of tuberculosis.[79] And like the men of the industrial age, a few women participated in numerous professional, political, and social activities. Mrs. John Blair's obituary identified her as "a business woman, civic leader, club woman, welfare worker, prominent Democrat and onetime suffrage leader."[80] Ten years following their inclusion in the political franchise, women fulfilled many varied roles in the public sphere as citizens who added to the country's well-being.

1910		**Women**	**Men**
	New York Times	15 percent	85 percent
	Chicago Tribune	18 percent	82 percent
	San Francisco Chronicle	18 percent	82 percent
1930			
	New York Times	18 percent	82 percent
	Chicago Tribune	17 percent	83 percent
	San Francisco Chronicle	32 percent	68 percent

Note: These percentages represent news obituaries only. The paid deaths listings in these sample weeks were chronicles of deaths containing no attributes of the deceased, only simple listings of names and funeral arrangements, and thus were not analyzed in this study. Children were represented in only a scattered few news obituaries, with their deaths included mainly in the paid deaths listings.

Political Influence

Mrs. Aaron Schloss
Feminist leader and Club Member Dies Near Berkeley, Cal.
Special to the New York Times

SAN FRANCISCO, Dec. 31—Mrs. Aaron Schloss, 64 years old, for more than a generation a leader in the feminist movement, died of heart disease yesterday at her new home in Orinda Park, Contra Costa, a suburb of Berkeley.

Mrs. Schloss was known for the campaigns she successfully conducted as president of the California Federation of Women's Clubs in 1920 and 1921 for a wife's community property rights in California.

New York Times, 1 January 1930

While only two women were noted for a political voice in the 1910 *Times* sample, numerous women in 1930 had political and social influence. In addition to women like Randolph, involved in health issues, and Mother Jones, a force in labor battles, the *Times* commemorated Mrs. Aaron Schloss as a leader in the feminist movement for more than a generation, "known for campaigns she successfully conducted" in California for women's community-property rights.[81] Elizabeth Clark was remembered as "one of the outstanding women orators of the country"; Dr. Sarah Kendall was recalled for taking "a prominent role in the campaign for woman suffrage"; and Fannie Bixby Spencer was noted for writing a controversial play promoting socialism.[82] Ten years after ratification of the Nineteenth Amendment, women were indeed making themselves heard in the political forum in a variety of ways and concerning numerous issues.

Some of the attributes reflected in women's obituaries in 1910 still lingered in 1930. For example, social prominence was still valued, with many women commemorated as members of "leading families." Longevity, as always, remained a notable virtue: the only acknowledged African American woman was identified as a "negress" and was included in the *Times* because, at age 109, she was believed to be the oldest person in Vermont.[83] And while being a native of a European country was often mentioned in 1910, the women who died in 1930 were more likely to be noted for being descendants of early American settlers.

Philanthropy

MRS. F. T. BRADBURY

Boston Philanthropist Dies—Helped Promote Health Work

Special to the New York Times

Mrs. Harriet J. Bradbury of Boston and Manchester, Mass., widow of Frederick Thomas Bradbury and sister of the late George Robert White, Boston philanthropist, died today.

Mrs. Bradbury, since her brother's death eight years ago, had devoted almost her entire time to further works of charity made possible by his bequest of $5,000,000 to the city. The income from this bequest is used in establishing health units throughout the city to promote health work.

New York Times, 5 April 1930

While wealth remained part of numerous women's obituaries in 1930, there was a distinct difference in its treatment. As the nation entered the Great Depression, the women of 1930 were noted more for the money they gave away than for wealth they possessed. Charity and philanthropy were among the most important attributes listed for women, perhaps because many were members of charitable clubs or women's associations. Mrs. Hugh Hamilton, for example, was acknowledged as the "most charitable person in Memphis," Lydia Titus was noted for donating money to hospitals, Sarah Elvira Colton was commemorated for giving land for a park, and Mrs. A. Naumburg was cited for donating $50,000 to a home for girls.[84] One woman philanthropist, an "exemplar of womanhood," according to her eulogy, was noted for "her devotion and love of myriads of human beings made happier and healthier by her constant unselfish service."[85] In times of intense financial anxiety, wealth was valued as a means to help others in the community.

Women commemorated in obituaries in the *San Francisco*

Chronicle and *Chicago Tribune* during 1930 closely resembled those in the *Times* in terms of occupations and acknowledged attributes, particularly philanthropic endeavors. The percentage of women in the *Tribune* decreased 1 percent from 1910, to 17 percent of the obituary total. Yet in the West, where suffrage had been more readily accepted, the *Chronicle* obituaries increased 14 percent to 32 percent of the total. As in 1910, the main differences in women's characteristics in the western newspapers were regional in emphasis, with western women remembered for being pioneers.[86] Obituaries in the California paper paid particular attention if the deceased woman had arrived in a covered wagon.[87] Surprisingly, in the Western papers, women in 1930 were more likely to be identified by their relationships to husbands and fathers than were women in the *Times* and were somewhat less likely to be referred to as being active in politics.

Uniquely American

GALESBURG, Ill.- (AP) - Mrs. Lucy Augusta Madison Corbett, 74, direct descendant of President James Madison's father and of John Hancock, died at the home of her daughter, Mrs. Frank A. Carpenter. Mrs. Corbett formerly was a resident of Rock Island.

New York Times, 4 January 1930

Links with American public memory for women in all three newspapers included mentions of their family lineage. The *Tribune* obituary for Mrs. M. E. Cabell is a good example. Not only was her father Abraham Lincoln's adviser and a Civil War hero, but her grandfather was an intimate friend of the Marquis de Lafayette, a symbol in revolutionary memory.[88] In the *Times*, Randolph was remembered in part for being the great-granddaughter of Thomas Jefferson, and Lizzie Offult Haldeman's obituary noted that "her ancestors were among the pioneers who accompanied Boone . . . over the wilderness trail."[89] Once again, those symbols so important to building a collective national memory, such as important events and male icons in American history, were important values in women's newspaper obituaries.

Industrial-Age Men

FREDERICK RENZIEHAUSEN

Distiller Who Made a Rye Whiskey Brand Famous Dies at 73

PITTSBURGH, May 31—Frederick C. Renziehausen, who in pre-prohibition days made rye whiskey of the Monongahela River Valley a world-famous product, died here yesterday at the age of 73. He was one of Pittsburgh's wealthy citizens.

He owned one of the model distilleries of the world. It is located at Large, Pa., near Clairton. Idle since the time when prohibition went into effect, it is estimated that the distillery holds 20,000 barrels of rye whiskey.

Mr. Renziehausen was born here. He was graduated from Western University of Pennsylvania. Five sisters and a brother survive. Mr. Renziehausen never married.

New York Times, 1 June 1930

Men's obituaries in the *New York Times* sample again represented a large portion, 82 percent, of the total obituaries published. In many respects, these obituaries resembled those published in 1910. The attribute still listed most often for a man was the number of years spent at work, even at a particular corporation. Many of these honorees were company founders who retired after many decades of work. The 1930 obituaries provided long lists of career promotions and appointments; recounted professional, civic, and athletic organizations; and mentioned the deceased's college or university affiliations, as in 1910. These men were often described as "prominent" or "well-known." Their occupations in 1930 also resembled those in 1910, including mostly upper management in major industries, founders or owners of smaller companies, entertainers, educators, physicians, journalists, and clergymen. Fewer government bureaucrats were commemorated than in 1910, and many of the men were retired.[90] But in the aftermath of a world war, more military officers were represented and service in the Civil War, Spanish-American War, and World War I were mentioned in numerous men's obituaries.

Like women in 1930, men who gave their money away after amassing large fortunes were noted for their philanthropy. For example, the *Times* commemorated W. H. Alford, a Nash automobile corporation executive, for his "benefactions," which were "estimated by friends to have totaled more than $1,000,000."[91] Another obituary praised a financier for giving more than $1 million to charity, and still another cited a railroad executive for being "one of the most public spirited men in his community."[92] Concern for the needy was a worthy enough attribute to warrant less wealthy men's inclusion on the obituary page. One policeman, for example, "won the affection of many unfortunates in [his] district because of many kindly acts that were never officially recorded," and another man was recalled for being the foster father of thirty-five children.[93] But despite the new emphasis on philanthropy, wealth was still an all-important attribute for *Times* men in 1930, just as it had been twenty years earlier. Owning a large amount of real estate or rising to a powerful corporate position remained noteworthy attributes.[94] And in an obituary that reflected both a concern for wealth and a nostalgia for the frontier, a former Texas Ranger was remembered for sleeping "under the stars, his saddle blanket his only bed" while he "dreamed of the agricultural development he later set in and made himself a rich man. . . . He was generally known as the 'Millionaire Sheriff.'"[95] Wealth indeed remained a virtue in 1930, but in this era of financial anxiety, those with money were remembered most fondly if they donated generously to the needy.

Ingenuity Remembered

The *Times* highlighted another attribute in 1930: ingenuity, perhaps another reflection of increasingly desperate financial times. A number of men were remembered as inventors, from the "creator of the stringless bean" to the inventor of the "penny-in-the-slot gas meter" to the man "credited with many inventions now in use in the modern typewriter."[96] George O. Page's obituary noted that he "rose from mechanic to successful inventor."[97] The *Times* called A. L. Riker an "inventive genius" for his work in the automobile industry and acknowledged W. H. Kelly's fame following his invention of a method of mixing lead and copper.[98] As jobs became increasingly specialized and automated, men who broke out of the mold with new ideas or products were worthy of commemoration in the *Times*.

Accomplished African American Men

REV. DR. W. D. COOK DIES

Negro Pastor of Chicago Church Had a Congregation of 4,000

CHICAGO, July 5—One of the outstanding members of Chicago's Negro community, the Rev. W. D. Cook, pastor of the People's Community Church of Christ, with a membership of 4,000, died today at his home, after an illness of nine months. His age was 71.

Dr. Cook was actively engaged in the ministry of the Methodist Episcopal Church for fifty-one years. He was a graduate of Shaw, Wilberforce and Howard Universities.

New York Times, 6 July 1930

Pana Pays Last Rites to Noted Negro Barber

Pana, Ill, March 31—(AP)—One of the largest funerals ever held here was that of John Wesley McCann, 78, a Negro barber and veteran of the civil war, being with Sherman on his march to the sea, held yesterday at the African Methodist church. Hundreds of friends of all colors and creeds gathered at the church and cemetery to pay McCann tribute.

"Wes" McCann had glided his razor over the faces of many notables of the United States in the years gone by, including Col. Robert G. Ingersol, "Marse Henry" Watterson, the noted southern editor; William Jennings Bryan, the late Senator Shelby M. Culom, the late Col. Dick Oglesby, former governor of Illinois and others.

Chicago Tribune, 1 April 1930

The *Times* obituaries in 1930 showed another noteworthy development, the increased inclusion of African Americans for their professional accomplishments rather than for longevity or a connection with a patriotic symbol. Though extremely sparse in number, these men represented a new kind of black worthy of commemoration in the mainstream press. For example, the *Times* noted the pastor of a

4,000-member Church of Christ, the Reverend Dr. W. D. Cook, as "one of the outstanding members of Chicago's Negro community," cited Rufus Lewis Perry as a "Negro attorney who embraced the Jewish faith," and remembered Edward H. Wright as a "power in Republican politics."[99] As with women in 1930, the newspaper's inclusion of African American men on the obituary page may have been statistically rare, but the content within those few obituaries changed and reflected a dominant culture slightly more willing to include African Americans who achieved status in their profession.

1910	**Women**	**Men**
	Associations with men, particularly accom-plished businessmen	Professional accomplishments
		Wealth
	Social prominence	Long years at work
	Wealth	Associations
	Personality	University education
	Beauty	Being well-known
	Being well-known	Prominent
	Contributing in social work, religious work and literature (a few)	Being an authority
		Age
	Pioneer spirit in West	Millionaire
		Being a capitalist
		Pioneer spirit in West
1930		
	Associations with men, but more for their own occupations and social contributions	Long years at work
		Career promotions
	Political voice and influence	University education
	Social prominence	Associations
	Charity and philanthropy	Prominence
	Pioneer spirit in West	Being well-known
		Philanthropy
		Inventions
		Pioneer spirit in West

American Symbols

DEADWOOD DICK, WESTERN HERO, INDIAN FIGHTER, DEAD

Pony Express Rider Who Made History in Early Days Succumbs to Long Illness at 83

DEADWOOD, S.D. May 5 (AP)—Deadwood Dick, 83, pony express rider, Indian fighter and one of the last picturesque characters of the old West, died here today.

Hero of countless exploits of the Black Hills gold rush, Deadwood Dick, whose real name was Richard W. Clarke, was a familiar figure in fact and fiction of the history-making period of the early days, claiming the acquaintanceship of "Wild Bill Hickok," "Buffalo Bill," Captain Jack Crawford, "Poker" Alice Tubbs and "Calamity Jane."

With his death the Black Hills lost the last of the famous characters who fought, gambled and dug for gold in the frontier days when the "Wild West" lived up to its name. "Poker Alice," queen of the gambling halls, died a few months ago.

Deadwood Dick died with his boots off. Survivor of the rigors of pioneer life, he lived to become a tradition in the decades that followed the passing of the stagecoach, the gold rush and the threat of Indian uprising. Weakened by old age, he for several years had been pointed out to tourists as the last living landmark of the old West. Early last year he made in airplane trip to Washington, where he was received by President Coolidge. It was the last long trip he made from the Black Hills.

He was born in Hansborough, England, December 15, 1845, and came to the United States when 16 years of age. Joining a party of prospectors in Illinois when a young man, Dick made the long overland journey to the Black Hills at the time when the excitement of gold discovery was at its height. During the years that followed he was a pony express rider, Indian fighter, guide and assistant to United States Marshals.

As Richard Clarke, he was connected with the stagecoach line that terminated at Deadwood, where his headquarters were for many years. Because of this he became known as "Deadwood Dick."

San Francisco Chronicle, 6 May 1930

The *Chicago Tribune* and the *San Francisco Chronicle* obituaries for men resembled those in the *Times* during 1930. Even the newspapers' references to pioneers were approximately equal in proportion, and the *Tribune* and *Chronicle* also commemorated long years of work, philanthropy, wealth, prominence, ingenuity, and associations with professional and social clubs. Perhaps in the years following U.S. participation in a world war, regional loyalty was not as important as national unity. In fact, links between obituaries and the historic events and symbols associated with American public memory were especially strong in the 1930 sample. The newspapers highlighted men for their associations with historic American symbols such as Lincoln, Buffalo Bill Cody, General Custer, General Sherman, Robert E. Lee, Mayflower Pilgrims, and Revolutionary settlers.[100] The newspapers pointed out three men who witnessed Lincoln's assassination personally from their seats at Ford's Theater, one of whom took up the chase for assassin John Wilkes Booth.[101] And all three newspapers published lengthy obituaries and photographs commemorating the death of the legendary Richard Clarke of Deadwood, South Dakota, known as "Deadwood Dick." Clarke was remembered as a Pony Express rider, Indian fighter, hero of the Black Hills gold rush, Wild West gambler, pioneer, stagecoach driver, and wilderness guide to U.S. marshals. His *Chronicle* obituary recalled that he was a "familiar figure in fact and fiction of the history-making period of the early days, claiming the acquaintanceship of 'Wild Bill' Hickok, 'Buffalo Bill,' Captain Jack Crawford, 'Poker Alice' Tubbs and 'Calamity Jane.'"[102] Obituaries during these sample weeks in 1930 spanned the public historical memory from the founding of the nation to the Wild West.

Career Cut Short

BOY CROESUS DEAD AT 17

Baltimore Youth, World's Richest Property Owner for Age, Succumbs

Career Cut Short

BALTIMORE, Feb. 4 (AP)—Seventeen-year-old Alan E. Lefcourt, probably the world's richest property owner of his age, died at the Baltimore Hospital yesterday of Anaemia. He was the son of A. E. Lefcourt, New York builder and real estate operator.

He had been under treatment at the hospital for the last month. Five years ago his father, who has built more than twenty five skyscrapers in New York, gave him a deed to 16,000 square feet of property at Madison avenue and Thirty-fourth street. Lefcourt at that time said he would erect a thirty-story building on the site, the total cost of the project being estimated at $10,000,000.

Lefcourt, in explaining his reason for turning the property over to his son, said he desired to turn the boy's attention to real estate and to train him in handling large real estate projects and thus be able to carry on his father's work. He said he wanted his son to have all the advantages denied him at the same age.

When the elder Lefcourt was 12 years old he was a newsboy and later proprietor of a shoe shining stand. He later entered the garment business where he acquired the money to finance his early real estate operations.

San Francisco Chronicle, 5 February 1930

The newspapers' mentions of the cause of death and funeral arrangements of men and women also closely resembled those in 1910, with heart attacks likely to draw the most attention. The obituaries often said that the funerals were to be "simple" but attended by large gatherings and pointed out that the deceased was not alone at the time of death. In addition to the telegraph, relatives could be summoned by radio and telephone.[103] An interesting new image, however, emerged in 1930, when numerous obituaries referred to death as the "end" or "closing" of a "career" rather than the end of a life.[104] One *Times* obituary, for example, carried the headline "Death Ends Career of Stock Junkman," and in the *San Francisco Chronicle*, the photograph of a seventeen-year-old who died of anemia carried the headline "Career Cut Short."[105] These metaphors indicate a society still obsessed with work and money.

A New American Century

The content of mainstream newspaper obituaries indeed changed during the twenty-year span that included ratification of the Nineteenth Amendment, with evidence of increased social inclusion by gender as well as reflectors of other major influences in American culture, including a world war and the beginnings of the Great

Depression. Increased inclusion was evident in the way obituaries were framed, in the selection, emphasis, and presentation of information published. For example, the percentage of women commemorated in all three newspapers may not have increased dramatically from 1910 to 1930, but those women who were remembered in 1930 were stronger, more powerful, and much more likely to be leaders, recognized as voices in the public debate over a variety of issues. Newspapers obituaries as part of news coverage indicate not only the increasing acceptance of women in political roles but also inclusion in many other arenas. These commemorated women worked in new careers and took the opportunity to speak out as voices of authority, and the newspaper, as part of the community and culture of the era, noted these accomplishments.

African Americans, sparse in numbers,[106] saw a change, too, with a few men commemorated in 1930 for their own professional accomplishments, not simply because they were extremely old or had some sort of connection to Lincoln, Washington, or Jefferson. This trend of inclusion did not extend to all groups, however. Asian Americans, for example, were noticeably absent from newspaper obituaries, especially in San Francisco, where many lived. Children were also virtually ignored in obituaries of both 1910 and 1930, though some were listed in the noncommemorative deaths columns that simply announced deaths and funeral arrangements.

Regional differences were stronger in 1910, before the world war, than in 1930, when many more obituaries linked individual citizens with historic events and major national symbols in public memory. American participation in a global conflict necessarily increased feelings of nationalism among individual citizens, who still vividly remembered that war rather than the fading regional conflict of the Civil War. Obituaries that signified a relationship between individual citizens and revolutionary patriots or frontier heroes promoted national unity and added to the dominant culture's stability. The framing of some obituaries, then, seemed to promote a social ideology of nationalism.

And as the nation moved from an era of intense industrial growth to the Great Depression, both men and women were likely to be remembered in 1930 more for their charitable contributions than for large estates, as in 1910. Wealth and industry, however, remained the most striking attribute in obituaries of both 1910 and 1930, indicating a capitalistic society that might have looked more to economic power than to political power as an indicator of what was worthy of remembering in a life. If an obituary legitimizes the life of a singular citizen, the citizen worth remembering in these eras was still a prominent white male. It seems likely that the virtual exclusion of poor men and women of European descent, African Americans, Native Americans, Asian Americans, and children resulted in large part to their lack of access to the higher levels of business and industry in this new American century.

THE FORGOTTEN DEAD

If Aristotle had been an obituary writer, he likely would have written about the deceased's strongest virtues and forgotten his or her occasional moral transgressions. Aristotle wrote of the constancy of virtues, that they do not follow changes of fortune but should be accessories of a person's life as a whole. "Among these [virtuous] activities . . . it is the most honorable which are the most permanent," he argued. "For that is apparently the reason why such activities are not likely to be forgotten."[1] A society, then, should tend to remember only the lasting virtues of its individual citizens, with obituaries providing an opportune place to commemorate the worth of each life as a whole while omitting and thus forgetting that person's unworthy attributes. Historically, the idea of death has helped people assess the value of their lives. Obituaries help in that life assessment by publishing the noteworthy attributes of individual lives, recalling for the public the virtues of deceased citizens. And just as the *Sun* deemed Baltimore businessman George C. Collins's death in 1855 a "public loss,"[2] so too were his and others' lives considered public models, instructing readers about worthy citizen attributes and actions.

Newspaper obituaries do more than simply chronicle basic facts about deaths; they also serve as commemorations and are invested with extraordinary significance.[3] Indeed, obituaries offer a vision of the ideal American life in different historical eras. But popular, mainstream newspapers certainly did not publish obituaries for every person who died in their respective cities, nor did they list every attribute of even those lives commemorated. In fact, in a democracy that extolls egalitarian values, many Americans have been excluded from obituary pages, and many attributes have been ignored. Were these lives deemed unworthy or somehow not representative of a social ideal? Such exclusions, whether deliberate or not, should offer still more insight into cultural values of these eras. Thus, in a study that focuses on increasing inclusion on obituary pages in American history, this chapter seeks to understand just who and what were forgotten.

Cathy N. Davidson, examining of the rise of the novel in America, reminds historians that "the omissions in a text are often as revealing as what the text explicitly tells. Yet it is difficult to formulate the rules whereby silence is admissible as historical evidence."[4] Obituaries are text, too, constructed fragments of history, tautological commodities meant for public consumption that are necessarily limited by constraints and professional norms of the dominant culture. Because obituaries deal both in virtues and in cultural relationships, the contributions of two renowned ethical/historical thinkers, one modern and one ancient, lend insight into who and what might have been forgotten. The writings of Aristotle, whose *Nicomachean Ethics* is a guide to living an ideal and virtuous life, aids in an examination of virtues. His classification of virtues and his "doctrine of the mean" have influenced ethical scholars for more than 2,000 years and help in determining certain social excesses and deficiencies deemed unsuitable for commemoration. And, second, any work that examines cultural exclusion could look at the debate inspired by the controversial historian and ethicist Michel Foucault, who wrote about power relationships in society.

The newspaper obituary, in fact, could be considered a battleground between ideas of these two theorists. By attempting to record the salient aspects of citizens' lives, the obituary would seem to celebrate individual virtues, to record what is unique and good about each life. But as a product of the dominant culture, the obituary would exclude some citizens and attributes and would subsume others into the mainstream culture. Of course, these theories are by no means all-inclusive. They are but two simple examples of how the merging of ethical theory and history might provide new windows to historical textual silences. Many other social observers' ideas and theories could offer still more information about who and what were excluded from mainstream American newspapers' obituary pages.

Newspapers have always worked to lure and keep audiences, attempting to give readers not only information deemed necessary but also information perceived as interesting or newsworthy. As newspapers became more mass publications and worked to appeal to the middle and lower classes as well as the elites, editors began publishing more sensationalized news. Those values crept into commemorative obituaries in rather surprising and interesting ways. These obituaries, though relatively sparse in number, offer occasional glimpses of forgotten groups.

Virtues played a major role in obituary coverage during the three time periods examined. Nineteenth-century obits spelled out those virtues by name, with deceased men described as *honest* or *courageous* and women as *pious* and *kind*, while twentieth-century obituaries were more likely to imply virtues through listings of the deceased's associations or accomplishments. Numerous mentions of the American Revolution, pioneer spirit, and links with historic events and symbols associated with American public memory indicate that virtues or other attributes considered uniquely American were especially important in all eras. In fact, what was remembered about the life of an individual might have more to do with the good of society than with the good of that individual. As Aristotle wrote, "For although the good of an individual is identical with the good of a state, yet the good of the state, whether in attainment or in preservation, is evidently greater and more perfect."[5] Individual traits not deemed virtuous from a social standpoint would likely be ignored. How, then, did Aristotle define virtue? "Virtue . . . is a state of deliberate moral purpose consisting in a mean that is relative to ourselves, the mean being determined by reason, or as a prudent man would determine it. It is a mean state firstly as lying between two vices, the vice of excess on the one hand, and the vice of deficiency on the other, and secondly because, whereas the vices either fall short of or go beyond what is proper in emotions and actions, virtue not only discovers but embraces the mean."[6] Though each man would seek and choose a mean relative to himself,[7] the virtues published in mainstream newspaper obituaries reflect a type of socially constructed "mean," a determined state lying between what a prudent man of the era would determine as excess and deficiency. As societies and cultural values change, so too do the ideals of the prudent man and that virtuous mean.

For a society that embraces egalitarianism, the ideals of virtue must be attainable for every citizen. Aristotle, discussing who can be virtuous, distinguishes between intellectual and moral virtues, "wisdom, intelligence and prudence being intellectual, liberality and temperance being moral."[8] Intellectual virtue, he argues, is a product of learning, while moral virtue comes from a lifetime of habit. Neither type of virtue, then, is "implanted by nature,"[9] but they develop during a lifetime; therefore, in an egalitarian society, each citizen should have the ability become virtuous and thus worthy of commemoration on the obituary page. But, of course, as the newspapers examined for this study indicate, many citizens' lives were not deemed worthy enough to be remembered. Taken individually, these omissions might not mean much. Information about the death of one worthy citizen, for example, might not have been available for newspaper editors, or another virtuous citizen's attributes might have been edited by family contributors, reporters, or even funeral directors before publication for any number of practical reasons having nothing to do with virtue. Taken collectively, however, and in context, trends of omission should provide telling information about moral and intellectual virtues and vices in the culture of any given era.

The moral and intellectual virtues designated by a culture likely would become apparent in the "attributes" category of information published in newspaper obituaries. But it would be naive to think that only citizens deemed immoral or nonvirtuous by Aristotelian standards were omitted from obits. Obituary pages—indeed, newspapers themselves—are texts representative of social relationships, which according to Foucault, are all about power. In a 1976 lecture, Foucault defined history, or "genealogy," as "the union of erudite knowledge and local memories which allows us to establish a historical knowledge of struggles and to make use of this knowledge tactically today."[10] These "struggles," including those evident in American newspaper obituaries, concern the relationships of power among human beings. Foucault spoke in an interview about these relationships, "whatever they are—whether it be a question of communicating verbally, or a question of a love relationship, an institutional or economic relationship—power is always present: I mean the relationships in which one wishes to direct the behavior of others."[11] Through their practice of inclusion and exclusion and their publication for a mass audience, obituaries likely helped direct social behavior, values, and attitudes, albeit subtly, by reflecting for a mass audience who held the power in society and what that power meant for others.

This, of course, does not mean that obituaries are or have been used as tools for social control. All the relationships—the deceased to family, family to community, newspaper editor to community and family, the living to the dead—are far too complex. Foucault called the individual a "product of a relation of power exercised over bodies, multiplicities, movements, desires, forces . . . the fictitious atom of an 'ideological' representation of society." But for Foucault, power should not always be described just in terms of exclusion because "power produces," he wrote, "it produces reality; it produces domains of objects and rituals of truth. The individual and the knowledge that may be gained of him belong to this production."[12] Obituaries for individuals could only serve to illustrate such ideological representations of society.

Timothy Wilson sums up Foucault's ideas about power and how they relate to history and the historian: "The past is not allowed to arise in any other manner than as a set of power relations."[13] For some historians, the newspaper obituaries could be viewed as simply another set of texts that—if examined in terms of power struggles among citizens, their powerful commemorative nature, and relationship to public memory—aid in an understanding of how power manifested itself as values during different eras in American culture. Foucault studied madness, specifically those people designated as being apart from the mainstream culture, and remarked that humanity is "bent on overhearing something in madness that could tell the truth about the human."[14] So, too, those who were excluded from obituary commemorations, those set apart from the dominant culture, might offer some truth of their own. The result, as Foucault might argue, is not necessarily a way to suppress that power, which is essential in the structure of a society, but a way to understand it, manage it, and make it more bearable.[15]

Those Forgotten

The first category of obituary information, the name and occupation of the deceased, serves as the likeliest indicator of whether a person would be remembered on the obituary page, and so it offers the simplest and most obvious clues about exclusion. Simply put, the nonelite were typically omitted. *Niles' National Register* in 1838 published a story following the death of Native American Osceola that illustrates the newspaper's usefulness as a tool for understanding those set apart from the dominant culture. Unlike obituaries published during the era, which commemorated remembered virtues of citizens, this news article was set apart and described Osceola's death, it explained, because it had often "graphically portrayed" his life, history, and personal appearance: "We are not of those who affect any overweening sympathy for the fortunes of the Indian race, or extravagant admiration of their character. . . . Of their inferiority, intellectually speaking, to the whites there can be no doubt—and their destiny, therefore, has been of necessity that of subjection to us."[16] Indeed, rare obituaries commemorating Native Americans in the nineteenth century were included only to illustrate that subjection. Mingo Mushulatubbee, for example, a Choctaw chief, was remembered because "his voice was often heard in council on behalf of the whites, and he led several parties of Choctaws against enemies of the United States in campaigns of Gen. Jackson." His life was remembered, as his obituary noted, because "he was a strong friend of the whites till the day of his death."[17] His noteworthy "virtue," then, would have been "justice," which, according to Aristotle, is a supreme state in which a fair man keeps the law "in relation to his neighbors."[18] Mushulatubbee was remembered for keeping and protecting the law, but, as Foucault might point out, it was the law of the dominant society, and his "neighbors" were the dominating white men. His obituary serves as an apt reflector of the relationships of power during the era. Likewise, a "Mrs. Mills," daughter of the chief of the Marquesas Islands, married an American missionary and was remembered for helping spread the "spiritual and temporal" ideas of the white Christian culture among the Marquesans: "Mrs. Mills, although a savage by birth, was a modest and well appearing woman, and her features were decidedly prepossessing."[19] Deaths of the vast majority of other Native Americans during the Jacksonian and Civil War eras went unnoticed in these mainstream publications, which venerated time and again the lives of "pioneers" who supplanted Native American culture and of the descendants of those pioneers. By the early twentieth century, when illustrating this subjection was no longer necessary, Native Americans were all but absent from obituary pages.

Likewise, deaths of nineteenth-century African Americans were virtually ignored in these mainstream publications.[20] Those few who were remembered seemed to have been included only because the deceased personified some type of news or cultural value. Longevity, for example, an important attribute in obituaries for all eras examined, was one way an African American obituary was chosen for inclusion: people who lived past one hundred were newsworthy.[21] A long life, as Aristotle might say, would be a means of achieving dignity and wisdom unique to that person, and "experience" would denote "a sort of courage."[22] Another avenue to commemoration on the obit page was any kind of link with American public memory. For example, Mr. Tucker Coles, "a Negro," was remembered for longevity and for having shaken hands with Thomas Jefferson, and John Blake was cited for speaking with officers at the battle of Brandywine during the American Revolution.[23] And just as with Native Americans, subjection was a noteworthy attribute. One "wealthy colored woman," for example, was remembered for having warned a planter about a slave conspiracy against his life.[24] These obituaries offer strong evidence of the importance of a dominant white culture in nineteenth-century America. As Paul Connerton argues in *How Societies Remember*, images of the past "commonly legitimate a present social order."[25] The only non-Caucasians commemorated in obituaries, published fragments of history, were people who in no way threatened that social order. And though more African Americans were commemorated during the suffrage era, these same types of obituaries continued into the twentieth century.

The importance of wealth and power in America is evidenced by omissions of the poor and powerless from obituary pages in all eras. Again, the news and cultural values associated with a long life and American public memory offer glimpses of the omissions by bringing in a few nontraditional obituaries, such as the one published in 1910 for Mary Ross, who died at 104 in an almshouse in Schenectady.[26] This obituary, likely published because of the deceased's longevity, was the only one from any of the sample years examined that mentioned a residence of this type or the receipt of any kind of social welfare, though numerous men and women were remembered for their kindness to the needy.[27] As Aristotle noted, liberality is a virtue, the liberal person being one who gives the right amount at the right time to the right person for the right motive.[28] Having financial resources to help the poor was worthy of commemoration, but being in need meant virtual exclusion. And although the Reverend Charles A. Cummings was remembered for his work with inmates in the county jail and was dubbed "the jailbird's friend" in his obituary in the *Tribune*,[29] not one of the more than 8,000 obituaries examined in this study mentioned a person dying in jail. The lives of most poor or socially outcast people, such as prisoners, and even the lives of most working-class people were absent from obituary pages in these major regional newspapers.

Children, too, were poorly represented in nineteenth-century newspaper obituaries and were virtually absent in the twentieth century. The 1855 *New York Times*'s "Deaths" column included 28 percent children, the highest percentage of any era examined, and 8 percent in news obituaries. Few attributes were listed even for those who were remembered.[30] This was an era, according to Gary Laderman, when mortality rates for children were extremely high. In fact, in the years just before the Civil War, between one-fifth and one-third of all children died before age ten, and some historians estimate the infant mortality rate at two hundred per thousand live births.[31] Based on these mortality rates, children could have dominated newspaper obituaries in the mid-1800s. By the turn of the century, mortality rates for children had dropped dramatically as a result of improvements in medical science,[32] but children remained noticeably absent from the 1910 and 1930 obituaries examined. Why were they not remembered? Aristotle might say they had not lived long enough to attain a virtuous life, to achieve a dignity, wisdom, and experience that would denote "a sort of courage."[33] But Foucault would likely contend that "power produces . . . reality; it produces domains of objects and rituals of truth."[34] For the most part, children, who lacked in social power, were not commemorated, their worthy attributes not recalled for the public in newspaper obituaries.

Likewise, only one obituary in any of the eras examined mentioned a physical disability not incurred through gallantry in battle. Dina E. Munger Sprague, who died at 101, had only been blind and deaf during the last few years of her life. She, too, was remembered for longevity and for the fact that her maternal grandfather was an officer in Washington's army.[35] Shared knowledge or memory, according to Geoffrey Hartman, is an "important yet often unconscious influence on personal identity,"[36] and collective values certainly influenced what was commemorated in Sprague's life.

Shared values also likely influenced the omission of disabled citizens, or at least any mention of their disabilities, from newspaper obituaries. Those people would not serve as ideological representations of the dominant culture.

The lives of women were commemorated in much lower percentages than their male contemporaries during all the eras examined, though women gained ground in sample years after all three political and cultural turning points. Most women recalled in newspaper obituaries were identified by relationships with men. Few single women of marrying age were included, unless, of course, their obituaries represented news or cultural value. Foucault's notions about the power relationships in a culture certainly hold true in mainstream newspaper obituaries, which highlighted the importance of wealthy white men in America.

Attributes Excluded

Attributes of deceased citizens, the next category of obituary information, also provide clues about exclusions from death stories. During the nineteenth century, obituaries listed deceased citizens' character traits, and based on the writings of Aristotle about the virtue of the mean, these commemorations offer glimpses that might help historians speculate about the social vices or taboos that were left out. In fact, one obituary, published in 1855 in the *New York Daily Times*, illustrates that ideal of vice being an excess or deficiency with virtue situated somewhere in between. Judge Herman Knickerbacker was commemorated for his dignity, hospitality, courtesy, wit, patriotism, and genius. But, as his obituary stated, "There were many faults as well as many virtues in his character, yet were his faults chiefly those which sprang from his peculiar virtues. Too much generosity and openness of heart often leads to a censurable improvidence—and a too brilliant social life oft usurps the time requisite for the attainment of the virtue of a thoughtful prudence."[37] Thus, being loose with resources and imprudent were considered social vices in Knickerbacker's America.

Pre-Jacksonian male virtues most often mentioned during 1818 were either public (patriotism, bravery, gallantry, vigilance, boldness, merit as an officer, honesty, skill, industry, zeal, devotion to duty, public esteem, and ardor) or private (dignity, hospitality, benevolence, good sense, integrity, kindness, and gentlemanly deportment). Aristotle discusses several of these virtues, as well as their corresponding vices, offering, for example, cowardice and foolhardiness as the excess and deficiency of courage.[38] Based on the idea of a socially constructed mean, distinct in each era, attributes considered unworthy of commemoration in 1818 might have included a lack of patriotism, cowardice, foolhardiness, dishonesty, imprudence, laziness, meekness, lack of skill, stinginess, and an unwillingness to fight for country, to name a few. Men who displayed these "vices" could do no good, public or private, and would serve as poor models for a people trying to define their national character and to gain a sense of economic security. These era "vices" would run counter to the building up of the nation, so important to the dominant culture during the national period.

Women's virtues in 1818 differed substantially from those commemorated for men of the era. These early-nineteenth-century women were described in domestic terms as patient, resigned, obedient, affectionate, amiable, pious, gentle, virtuous, intelligent, educated, tender, innocent, and useful. Again, using the idea of a socially constructed era mean, those attributes left out of obituaries were either the excess of those virtues or their deficiency. To borrow a few possibilities from Aristotle, that list might include impatience, meanness, vulgarity, conceit, irascibility, sullenness, surliness, disobedience, illiteracy, roughness, and guile.[39] Women who were cold and discourteous or uncooperative were not worthy of commemoration. These speculative "vices" reflect an era when subjection to those with power was not limited to the poor or people of color. Women of 1818 who were commemorated were most often identified by their relationships with men and displayed only virtues that would support those men.

As the nation grew, virtues listed in obituaries for both men and women changed. During the next sample year examined, 1838, men were remembered less for patriotism than for their business and social attributes; this trend continued through the Civil War era. Vices, then, for men might have been those qualities that would stand in the way of the rise in industry. Men who were bankrupt or who were not frugal, for example, would be unworthy of commemoration, as would those who were lazy or weak or who lacked commercial skills. These men would be ignored—or at least those attributes would not be mentioned in obituaries. Again, women were the helpmates of men, and those women who were ostentatious or uncooperative were not mentioned—or at least those negative attributes were ignored.

After the turn of the century, character traits that reflected Aristotelian virtues were seldom listed but were implied through associations and good works. The work ethic became a man's most important virtue, again suggesting that laziness or lack of industry and initiative might be the most unforgivable vices. Work and industry became so important that many obituaries for women listed in great detail their husbands' or fathers' career achievements, giving little to no information about the possible worthy attributes of the deceased women. Women's social prominence was the virtue that made them valuable to the dominant culture, because it was likely the attribute that helped their men succeed in business.

Examining obituaries over time offers insight into how society struggles with changing attitudes about a particular virtue or vice. For example, nineteenth-century obituaries were filled with commemorations of Christian piety for both men and women. Many were like that of a New York woman who died in 1870 and whose obituary stated, "If a pure and useful life is beautiful, and if an exemplary Christian life is worthy to be held in remembrance, it is fitting that we should yield a passing tribute to the memory of Eliza Vredenburgh Porter."[40] But what happened at the death of a noteworthy person who was not an example of piety, a person who was known for rejecting the Christian faith? Nineteenth-century newspapers examined offer evidence of a society struggling with such a question. One man who died in 1838 was "not a professor of the religion of Christ." But his obituary assured readers, "He was, however, a liberal supporter of its institutions; he was a man of unbending principle."[41] Another man died without having made any "public professions of religion," but his obituary, too, reassured readers that "he was nevertheless duly impressed with the great truths and consoling benefits of Christianity."[42]

A number of Jewish citizens were commemorated in obituaries during the Civil War and suffrage eras, if references to temples or Jewish organizations are an indication, but no references were made to the strength of their faith.[43] References to Christianity and sentimental religious rhetoric, however, began to decline after the Civil War. Christianity was seldom mentioned by 1910 or 1930, unless the deceased was, for example, a minister or missionary, but religious affiliations were sometimes listed. The virtue of religious piety, so important in the Jacksonian era that it dominated obituary columns, had all but disappeared a century later.

Divorce, as a reflector of vice, also experienced a metamorphosis in the newspaper obituaries examined. For Aristotle, marital fidelity would represent a desirable mean, and virtuous husbands and wives would delight in that union and in their families.[44] It is not surprising, then, that during the nineteenth century, mentions of divorce were virtually absent from obituary pages. Most adult citizens commemorated were married; if not, they were pitied, as was Professor Joseph Keany, who was called "unfortunate" because he was single.[45] By 1910, a more sensationalist press would sometimes include salacious tidbits about the deceased's domestic woes. One senator's obituary recounted his undoing in public opinion: "Senator Platt's later years were embittered by domestic troubles . . . The marriage [to Lillian T. Janeway] was not harmonious, and in 1906 the two separated, each making allegations against the other. Scarcely had the two become legally separated when Platt was sued for divorce by Miss Mae Wood, who had been at one time his stenographer at Washington. Although the marriage was never proved, it was shown that the Senator and his stenographer had been very intimate."[46]

When the famous architect Frank Lloyd Wright's ex-wife died, her obituary noted their tumultuous divorce, when she "stormed the gates [of their home] followed by a number of newspaper men and curious onlookers" and "threw things at the guards who had been posted to keep her off the property."[47] By 1930, however, some obituaries simply referred to former wives in obituaries and listed them among survivors without scandalous details. Divorce was more prevalent in the dominant culture but remained an issue of social debate, as indicated by the obituary of the Reverend Dr. George Elliott, said to be President Grover Cleveland's favorite pastor. Elliott was known for relaxing Methodist bans against card playing, dancing, and theatergoing, but he stood firm on the issue of divorce. As his obituary noted, Elliott argued, "even if a person does suffer in marriage by cruelty or brutality, Christians have learned they must suffer."[48] Divorce, excluded as a social vice from nineteenth-century obituaries, could not be ignored in the early-twentieth-century sensationalist press: though controversial, divorce moved closer to social acceptance.

One important attribute, or virtue, that remained constant throughout all three eras was living a long, sturdy, and vigorous life. Longevity, of course, was noteworthy attribute of obituaries of both centuries, but so, too, was being vigorous up to the end. Victorie Simon Mercier died at the age of 111 and was noted for remaining "active and sensible to the last." As her obituary noted, "On Friday last she walked a distance of three squares."[49] Another woman had attended church on her hundredth birthday and had been "about house until a few days before her death," and her obituary remarked that her ninety-eight-year-old brother could still "do a good day's work at haying."[50] And Josiah Zeitlein, called Brooklyn's oldest man, died at 106 after "never knowing a day of illness." His obituary gave an account of his daily ritual: "Mr. Zeitlein occupied a room on the top floor of the four-story house, and each night would climb unaided the three flights of stairs. He arose early each morning and after swallowing some strong tea, would take several drinks of whisky. He would then smoke two pipes full of tobacco and go back to bed. Later in the day he would get up again and repeat his performance. He was always healthy and cheerful and never used eyeglasses." The *New York Times* concluded the Brooklyn man's obituary by quoting his secrets for longevity, which were never eating quick lunches, eating little meat, sleeping eight hours a day, and never visiting doctors. "When you reach the age of ninety years you may do about as you please," advised the deceased.[51] Obituary pages, though concerned with disease and death, extolled the virtues of living a full life and thus minimized those citizens whose mental and physical health did not allow them to personify this virtue.

The Deaths

The third category of obituary information, cause of death, also suggests some exclusions from the obituary pages in all three eras. When medical science took hold in the United States in the mid- to late nineteenth century, obituaries began listing more specific causes of death.[52] In 1855, just prior to the Civil War, obituaries were filled with death imagery and graphic causes. That phenomenon declined dramatically after the war, when scholars argue that Americans began turning away from death as a subtle symbol of patriotism.[53] But were some causes of death taboo? And can those "silences" on the obituary pages reveal something about social vices or power relationships?

With rare exceptions, murder was not listed as a cause of death in any era examined, though the homicide rate in cities in the mid–nineteenth century was approximately 4 per 100,000 people and by 1930 had increased to nearly 9 per 100,000 people.[54] Early-twentieth-century obituaries sometimes went out of their way to assure readers that the deceased was not a victim of homicide: "The theory that [James] Crane was murdered by thugs," one obituary noted, "is dispelled by the fact that his money, watch and jewelry had not been taken from his pockets. There are no marks of violence on the body other than that of the fracture of the skull." Despite this injury, Crane was said to have died of apoplexy, his fracture the result of a fall.[55] One short news story, published to clear up a possible discrepancy from an earlier account, offered an "official denial that Joseph Miguiel . . . died as a result of a beating in a free-for-all fight." The hotel proprietor's cause of death, too, was listed as apoplexy.[56] Whether the dominant culture was uncomfortable with the idea of violence as a reminder of the somewhat fragile nature of social power, or whether the victims of murder were somehow unworthy of commemoration, murder was all but absent from newspaper obituaries, though it remained a consistent element of front-page news stories.

Just as piety and divorce offer evidence of a society struggling with changing values, so too does suicide as a cause of death in obituaries. Suicide has been a part of news coverage in both centuries, though people who killed themselves in the 1800s were not commemorated on the obituary pages, at least in the newspapers examined for this study. News stories about suicides, estimated at nearly 5 per 100,000 people during the era,[57] were published apart from obituaries. For example, when William McConnell shot himself in the head after killing a slave, the *Baltimore Sun* printed lengthy details, and the story about the shooting suicide of McKendry Weaver, who had been "unusually melancholy," included his suicide note.[58] Yet neither article included attributes of the deceased or the funeral arrangements. But by 1910, when the suicide rate was approximately 15 per 100,000 people,[59] the newspapers examined indicated an uneven response to treatment of these deaths. Some suicides were published strictly as news stories, others ran alongside obituaries but included no funeral arrangements or attributes, and suicides were occasionally printed in an "Obituary Notes" column.[60] By 1930, on rare occasions suicides were published as traditional obituaries with attributes, funeral arrangements, and a more compassionate treatment of the death. For example, the obituary for Thomas A. Ross of Berkeley, who hanged himself in the basement of his home, told readers that despondency over ill health was the cause and then noted his prominence in fraternal circles and immigration to America from Australia.[61] Philip McDermott, who jumped from a sixth-floor hospital window, was described as a "graduate of New York University and a war veteran."[62] Still, in 1930, newspapers were likely to sensationalize or deny suicide. May Alexandra Crocker, a "divorcee," inhaled gas in the kitchen of her apartment, and though her obituary printed funeral arrangements for her family and friends, it also pointed out that she "was wearing expensive jewels and an evening gown when she sat down in an easy chair after opening five jets on the gas range."[63] Artist Patrick Tuohy's death was reported as a suicide in the 4 September 1930 *New York Times*, which speculated the cause as despondency over an injury, but two days later the *Times* retracted the story, saying the cause of death had been ruled accidental.[64]

Suicide, according to Aristotle, represents not only harm to self but injustice to the state, which does not voluntarily sanction the loss. It is worse to commit injustice, he wrote, than to suffer it.[65] Newspapers of both the nineteenth and twentieth centuries, fascinated by stories of death, struggled with how to relate details of those deaths without promoting a social injustice or somehow empowering those who set themselves apart from society. Information about citizens who committed suicide in both centuries offer evidence of an American society intolerant of illness, weakness, loneliness, or despondency.

Funerals

The final category of obituary information, funeral arrangements, also offers a few clues about social exclusion. Funerals of prominent citizens, especially in the early Jacksonian era, were described at length, while the newspapers ignored people of more modest means. Descriptions of funerals sometimes served as lessons. Cherokee Richard Brown, commemorated for his aid to General Andrew Jackson and his efforts toward a settlement of a treaty in Washington, D.C., was said to have been interred "with military honors, amidst a very numerous and respectable assemblage."[66] His funeral served as an example of his subjection and his worth to the dominant white culture. The funeral procession of one wealthy man who died in 1870 was attended by "not less than 10,000 people . . . persons representing all classes, and the windows of neighboring dwellings were filled with spectators."[67] He, too, served as a public example in death, an illustration of the deference of lower classes to the wealthy.

A few obituaries also offered clues about changing religious values, especially in twentieth-century America. Most obituaries that described funerals after the fact spoke of Christian services, with some even quoting sermons and listing hymns. Other obituaries of both eras spoke of "simple ceremonies" conducted by ministers, followed by burial. But obituaries or news stories occasionally told of the unusual, a non-Christian service or a nontraditional way of dealing with remains. Captain A. R. Simmons was said to be "a firm believer in evolution" who "expressed the further desire that no religious services be held over his body and that his friends in performing the last rites conduct themselves with as much gaiety as possible."[68] Moses A. Harmon, an advocate of free thought, asked that his body be turned over to physicians for instruction in anatomy, but his daughter could find no physicians who wanted to "take advantage of that strange bequest. . . . Consequently funeral services will be held . . . and the body will be cremated." As the headline "Daughter to Burn Body of Noted Free Thinker" indicates, the *San Francisco Chronicle* considered the fate of Harmon's remains newsworthy.[69] Although Christianity was seldom mentioned as a virtue in twentieth-century obituaries, most deceased citizens were still expected to have sober, religious burials. Those who chose other options were considered oddities.

The Silences

As this study indicates, many American citizens have been excluded and many attributes ignored on mainstream newspaper obituary pages. Based on Aristotle's ideas concerning virtue ethics and Foucault's beliefs about construction of the Other in a culture built on power relationships, these silences or omissions offer clues about American press values and about the sense of the worth of a singular life in society. Obituaries, because of their commemorative nature, gave newspapers the opportunity to promote virtue—or at least a type of virtue that represented a socially constructed Aristotelian mean of the era. Whether editors were cognizant of this role is unknown, though evidence suggests that they believed in the obituary's worth as a model for citizens to emulate. Foucault would reiterate that obituaries are simply texts that represent relationships of power in a society. So the same obituaries that represent a type of social virtue also exclude many Americans, including the poor, minorities, social outcasts, and many women and children. These excluded people and their attributes were certainly real but were somehow deemed unworthy of commemoration. Thus, the value of these people's lives, which might have been recorded for the public in the mass press, was lost to American collective memory.

"IN THE MIDST OF LIFE"

The *Daily National Intelligencer*'s obituary for William Custis, the "noble, independent and honest" Virginia businessman who died in 1838, served multiple purposes. It informed newspaper readers of Custis's death, recalled what was deemed worthy about his life, and served as a model so "that his name should not be left in oblivion, nor his influence be lost."[1] Custis's obituary, which appeared in a popular and respected newspaper, legitimized publicly this citizen's life. More than a century and a half later, his obituary still serves as a type of model by providing clues about the culture of his America, about the value of an individual citizen's life in the formative years of the nation. Taken collectively and in context, historic newspaper obituaries paint a picture of the "ideal" American man and woman, which changes based on society's needs.

Newspaper obituaries, which have been part of American newspaper coverage since the nation's birth, included specific types or categories of information—the name and occupation of the deceased, the attributes of the deceased, the cause of death, and the funeral arrangements. During the Jacksonian, Civil War, and suffrage eras, when the United States was becoming more inclusive politically, each of these categories offered information not only about the individual but also collectively about the changes in American culture. Obituaries show how Americans viewed death and, perhaps more important, how they valued the singular American life. These obituaries provide a unique window to examine changing American culture because they offer a rare link between the average citizen and the society. Obituaries show new inclusiveness in the lives legitimized and recounted and depicted specific values in nineteenth- and twentieth-century America.

Uniquely American

Obituaries reflect the worth of a life. Because of their link with American public memory and because of their presence in the mass media, obituaries make an important contribution to American society's well-being. A society requires a shared memory, and obituaries help fulfill that need. For American society, shared memory has focused in part on cultural symbols associated with the country's history: the American Revolution, the rugged explorer-adventurer, the sturdy pioneer, and the rags-to-riches immigrant businessman. Obituaries reinforce those important public symbols by referring to their value in the remembered lives of individual citizens. What was considered worthy of commemoration in an individual's life often was some sort of connection to one of these national symbols. For example, the deceased did not have to be George Washington for the obituary to promote national pride and unity. All this person needed was to have sold Washington a book or performed for him in a choir. Any association with the hero Washington was a connection to the revolution and the founding of the nation. During the Jacksonian era, as America grew and egalitarian values flourished, the deceased did not have to be Davy Crockett, hero of the everyman, but could be likened to him through rugged individualism and daring. That association with Crockett or Daniel Boone was a connection to American expansion.

During the early twentieth century, a pioneer harness maker and pioneer banker were still American pioneers, even if they did not travel west in a covered wagon. By a stated association with American symbols, these people could be part of the great American history, too, their remembered lives serving a need for a shared national memory. In an egalitarian society, obituaries become an important link between everyday citizens, as valued members of the democracy, and those American icons. Generations after the passing of Washington and other heroes of the American Revolution, their memory had a respect, a value, that remained part of obituary coverage. In the early twentieth century, descendants of the revolutionary patriots were acknowledged in their obituaries, thereby promoting national unity. Through mass press obituaries, such important relationships between individual citizens and national symbols are publicly acknowledged.

Cultural Guidance

Obituaries are powerful commemorations that focus on social values. True, they are important to family and friends of the deceased, but they also provide information and cultural guidance for a larger society by revealing how individuals adhere to various cultural norms. Throughout American history, the mass press made that influence increasingly national in scope because, from the earliest newspapers examined, citizen obituaries reached far beyond their hometowns. Newspapers in the Jacksonian era regularly exchanged copies, and many obituaries included notices indicating that the articles had been reprinted from exchange papers. Local obituaries, too, often included notes at the bottom asking newspapers in specific towns to copy and publish the information. During the Civil War era, the telegraph was such a new technological innovation that newspapers proudly published anything received by wire, including obituaries of citizens from far-off cities, even if that person was not well-known to a national audience. In the twentieth century, the rise of wire services such as the Associated Press enabled obituaries to reach a national audience, especially notices commemorating well-known Americans or containing some sort of news or cultural value.[2] Obituaries that included worthy attributes and actions of the deceased reinforced accepted values, not only for a local community but also for an increasingly national community, providing another element of American unity.

Memories and history are not fixed things, of course, but are mere representations or constructions of reality that can change based on present needs. Obituaries represent the dominant society by revealing a type of conformity of individual citizens. Those who remain apart from the dominant culture are remembered only if they serve some sort of purpose, such as to reinforce subjection or illustrate a news or cultural value, or if they have one trait so powerful as to prevent its being ignored. The unique individual, then, could be subsumed by the dominant society.

Death Stories

Obituaries are strong representations in part because of their commemorative nature and in part because they are death stories that invoke fascinating symbols of religion and ritual. Ernest Becker's *The Denial of Death* postulates that "the idea of death, the fear of it, haunts the human animal like nothing else; it is a mainspring of human activity—activity designed largely to avoid the fatality of death, to overcome it by denying in some way that this is the final destiny for man."[3] For most citizens, an obituary is the final public notice of an existence, the final bit of published instruction for society about that person's contributions and character that might live on after death. But unless specific instructions are left behind, rarely would the deceased have any real influence on what exactly is commemorated of his or her life. Those decisions have been left in the hands of family members or friends, newspaper reporters and editors, and, following the turn of the twentieth century, even funeral directors. In newspapers that charged for citizen obituaries, those decisions unfortunately may simply have been financial.

Though it is difficult to determine which of these groups or variables wielded the most influence over content, obituaries during all three eras studied indicate shared ideas about the worth of singular lives. In the nineteenth century, for example, obituaries promoted character traits such as courage or honesty, and in the twentieth a work ethic was the dominant value. Media framing devices within obituaries help scholars understand how these news stories taught the public about the social value of a life and about the way to deal with death. For example, the same words and types of phrases were used time and again to describe deceased men's and women's attributes. Nineteenth-century obituaries focused on character, with a worthy life nearly always framed as a virtuous one filled with gallantry for men and gentle piety for women. Twentieth-century obituaries often represented the individual's life as a long list of business or social associations and downplayed individual character. These obituaries offer a small glimpse into an America with distinctly different cultures in the nineteenth and twentieth centuries, the ideal American changing from a courageous, rugged individual to the man or woman whose value was reflected by associations.

The use of imagery associated with American public memory was also a framing device, a way to promote national unity. When the word *pioneer* appears in obituary headlines time and again, it is not a leap to infer the ideological importance of a pioneer ethic—in both its adulation of the courageous explorer and its subtle support of the conqueror in the dominant culture. The way obituaries framed the act of dying reveals, too, a cultural evolution in America. Men and women in the Jacksonian era met death without a murmur, bravely, while in the heart of the sentimental Victorian era they were visited by the "King of Terrors." Death was no longer something to use as a final witness, an example of Christian faith, but was fearful and unavoidable, worthy of obsession, something to struggle against. During the early twentieth century, however, as the public expression of Christianity waned in the dominant culture, death lost its sentimental significance. It was often presented simply as the end of a career, implying that somehow the value of a life was related to success in business in this industrial age: in death, business potential was the most important loss.

Ideal Americans

Obituaries can reflect greater social ideals while focusing on the lives of individual citizens and thus provide a truly intimate portrait of the "ideal American" in any era. Just who is that American man or woman? What does he or she contribute to society's well-being? Obituaries indicate that he or she changes with the times, that virtue is not stagnant but adapts to the new cultural demands of a changing society. These needs, for example, were naturally different in the national period, when America was building character, than at the beginning of the Great Depression, when economic instability required the ideal citizen's business acumen and ingenuity. So the ideal American commemorated in mainstream newspaper obituaries naturally represents the dominant culture and its values. Whether each individual depiction is accurate from a factual standpoint is irrelevant. For historians, it really does not matter, for example, if Virginian William Custis had sterling business principles: it matters that his published obituary presented him that way to the public. The ideal American of any era represents a social model, with virtues presented through the mass media for citizens to emulate.

Near the beginning of the Jacksonian era, the ideal 1818 American was a member of an elite who helped build the nation through his stately courage and patriotic service. He—and obituaries generally appeared only for men—was an intellectual who held a position of influence in the formation of the new government or was a leader in education or in a religious community. As America grew, struggling to define itself collectively, this man's unflinching character offered the promise of a strong and virtuous nation. He would provide reassurance that the new America would be undergirded by rational, virtuous, brave men capable of leading it into the future. This type of reassurance was much needed in an era when egalitarian rhetoric gained strength but when Americans were not entirely certain where this new egalitarianism would go. And while the ideal man built, protected, and reassured the nation with such an elite character, the ideal 1818 woman took care of the home, where the most perfect peace and harmony prevailed. Education was important for this gentle woman, for raising her children, for managing domestic concerns and serving as a pious example for her family. In death she embodied the Christian promise of salvation and eternal life. This woman did not seek fame; she was not at all ambitious of worldly show. Her worth was domestic and in a private sphere. She was innocent, obedient, and useful, all qualities that would serve well and assist the dominant male nation builder, her contemporary. Her attributes and roles, too, would reassure Americans about the stability and character of the new nation.

Following Andrew Jackson's election to the presidency in 1828, Americans embraced a type of egalitarianism, in theory at least, for all white men, the new inclusion defined in terms of male suffrage. But the ideal American in mainstream newspaper obituaries, regardless of gender, provides evidence of increasing social inclusion. The man commemorated in 1838 was more of an everyman. He was likely to be a clerk, bookseller, land registrar, printer, or physician, rather than a public servant or military officer, a builder of the new nation. He was remembered not so much for courage and gallantry as for attributes that would help him relate to others in his community, ensuring strength in the collective efforts. His individual character traits served that end. This ideal American was generous and kind, a devoted and warm family man whose home was always open and whose hospitality was always unostentatious. Obituaries still commemorated elite Americans, true, but elitism as an attribute was not revered in 1838. As America moved into the industrial age, the ideal man became more of a consummate businessman, intelligent, punctual, efficient, and frank in all his transactions. His amiability and integrity helped his business, and his generosity suggested that economic success was a product of and an opportunity for virtue, not necessarily a virtue in and of itself.

The new political inclusiveness of the era was limited by gender, of course, and the ideal woman of 1838 was still a pious example, devoted to domestic duty, and a gentle, kind helpmate to her businessman husband. While she remained modest and unobtrusive, an interesting change occurred in her character. The ideal woman of 1838 was admired and esteemed by all who knew her, which suggests subtly a public place for women, if not yet a political voice. It follows that a woman could not be admired by those outside the domestic circle without filling some sort of public role in the community for outsiders beyond her private sphere. Women of 1818 were given no such public admiration beyond the home. In the new, more egalitarian society of 1838, the ideal woman moved from a type of domestic obscurity to a place of esteem. While the Jacksonian-era man stepped down from his metaphorical pedestal, the ideal woman began taking tiny steps on that long climb upward.

Just prior to the outbreak of Civil War in America, the ideal 1855 male displayed different characteristics depending on where he lived. The New York man was esteemed for his intellect and strong character. He was manly, though courteous and kind, and he was patriotic, an attribute experiencing a resurgence as the nation entered a perilous era. But this man had a newly developed sense of humor—he could pause and laugh at himself, another virtue of the everyman. In the South, the New Orleans man displayed many of the same characteristics, though he was a "true gentleman" and not necessarily a patriot. Nobility, not nationalism, served his community. Here was a social man of ample means, brave, energetic, and firm. His humor was graceful, his manner sometimes boyish, and prophetically, he was calm in the face of death. In Baltimore, the ideal man was also of strong character, financially secure, and generous with his good fortune. He too was witty and brave. This ideal Baltimore man, however, supported the institution of slavery, but only if slave owners displayed similar strength of character. In a society about to rip apart, these ideal men represented in three mainstream newspapers indicate many shared values but offered hints of the rising rift to come. The New Orleans man, in direct opposition to his New York contemporary, began promoting a different kind of ideal, one that offered up the southern gentleman as a proper substitute for the patriot, regionalism as a substitute for nationalism.

The ideal woman of 1855 was a supporter of her husband, just as were her Jacksonian-era predecessors. Regionalism was not as important for her as for the ideal man of the era, though in the South the ideal woman was more vivacious and beautiful. No matter where she lived, however, this woman was valued as a Christian, gentle and obliging—an "esteemed servant" who never spoke ill of another. But in 1855 she was also talented and happy, a step forward from her ideal sister of just seventeen years earlier. Such talent indicates a new kind of public role for a woman because that talent would be recognized, and the woman could be known outside the private sphere. This ideal 1855 woman, however, still maintained a strong domestic role. A nurturer who took care of her husband and children, she was always ready to relieve distress in these most stressful of times. She contributed to society's well-being by offering comfort to a nation on the verge of collapse.

After the Civil War, the ideal man of 1870 was a product of his region. In New York he was a hero among heroes, a man whose noble service during the war held him in highest esteem. He was strong, partly as a result of his sturdy pioneer ancestry, was energetic, and could persevere through the most difficult of times. In short, he was a patriot, the savior of the republic. In New Orleans, the ideal man may have lost the war, but he kept his nobility and his worth as a true gentleman by living as a man of character and courtly manners. The man's extraordinary enterprise and his business capacity made him rich, despite the fact that his region had been ravaged, his city occupied. In 1870, bravery for the southern man was not about patriotism but about his community's economic survival. In Baltimore, a border city with its own unique perspective on the stresses of war, the ideal man got along with everyone, as was necessary to survive at that border. He was genial and, because of his ability to make friends, popular. He displayed characteristics that enabled his community to survive a perilous era. Of course, some virtues, such as kindness and integrity, remained common to all three regions. In all areas, the ideal man was still a Christian. He no longer focused on death with the same fervor as before the war. And he was a model businessman during this era when the nation strode quickly into the industrial age. In short, he was the kind of man who could help America recover and get back to the business of living.

Following the war, the ideal American woman had changed, too. While she was still a Christian, as sweet and useful as were her ideal sisters of 1855 and the Jacksonian era, this woman developed some new qualities. Death accounts now emphasized her strength and generosity. No longer was she simply a manager of domestic concerns; this new woman of 1870 had a public role. She was a leader who held a prominent position in fashionable society. She was also a straightforward woman with natural dignity who had the ability to succeed in public roles formerly held by men, as a writer or even a doctor. In the South, where money had become something of a preoccupation, she was noted for her charitable efforts and for her class standing. In Baltimore, she struggled with her new public role but was recounted as a woman of social standing, extensively known and beloved. The ideal American woman of 1870, then, no longer was required to relieve distresses and to be just a guardian of harmony in the home. She was a kind, Christian woman of economic prosperity whose social prominence was increasingly viewed as a reward for her husband's success.

Following the turn of century both the ideal man and women differed greatly. In 1910, he was a captain of industry, a man who founded and ran his own business while offering advice as a member of the boards of directors of numerous other corporations. No longer was he known for his character or specific virtues of courage and generosity. Rather, this new twentieth-century man was remembered for long lists of corporate affiliations, promotions, and appointments and for the size of his considerable estate. His wealth, his property, his accumulations were acknowledged. He was a man who believed in work, and he remained loyal to his corporation for decades, leaving only when his health failed or in death. His obituary acknowledged that he was college educated. In the West, he displayed a real pioneering spirit, either as a Forty-Niner or as an early leader in his profession. He was also a member of many professional and social clubs. Yet this ideal man was not perfect. In an era when the press focused more on sensational aspects of a life, he was now seen to have human frailties, publicly acknowledged. He might have experienced some domestic trouble, for example, or been involved in a political squabble, yet these flaws paled in the glow of his wealth and social esteem. He was the consummate capitalist during an era when builders of America were men of industry, wealth, and power. And he wielded that power for the public good, the nation's growth.

In a society so consumed by industrialization, it follows that the ideal woman of 1910 would be the wife, mother, sister, or daughter of one of those successful capitalist men. She resembled the ideal man of her era in that she no longer was known for traits of character, such as kindness or piety. Rather, she was remembered for her social prominence, evidence of her husband's or father's economic prosperity, and for her personality, which helped her navigate those social highways and made her well-known to other men and women of her monied class. Simply put, the ideal woman of 1910 was a rich wife, an elitist. And while she might be aware of a few of her contemporaries speaking out in social, education, or religious circles, she was not yet one of those women. Just as her ideal man, this woman of 1910 filled a role made possible and even necessary in a dominant culture obsessed with the acquisition of wealth.

By 1930, ten years after women achieved full citizenship by suffrage, the nation's economic prosperity had collapsed. Post–World War I prosperity had come and gone. The Great Depression raged, and the obituaries adapted to the values of an ideal man and woman of the era. The man of 1930 was still identified by his association with a major corporation, known for his many decades of service to that corporation and his long list of promotions and appointments. But the commemorated man of 1930 was much more likely to retire rather than to work until his health failed. He might still be wealthy, but he could not ignore the growing crisis of poverty around him. He generously contributed money to the needy, and in these times of economic peril, he displayed ingenuity by inventing new products that reassured his community of continued American success and prosperity. His obituary also mentioned that he was associated with those symbols of American public memory that promoted national unity and stability. For example, he was a man of revolutionary stock who headed west in his youth and knew intimately the heroes of the old frontier, such as Buffalo Bill Cody or Wild Bill Hickok. Or, he was a Forty-Niner, a participant in the California gold rush, before settling down to a worthy career in industry. This man indeed lent comfort and provided a sense of history and unity for a postwar society that was riveted by economic fear and despair.

In 1930, when jobs were scarce, the ideal woman was still strongly identified by an association with her ideal man, but surprisingly, in an era when married women were discouraged from work outside the home, she was much more likely to have an interesting, nontraditional job as well as a political voice. She was an acknowledged expert and even a crusader for rights of women and laborers. She was of good family stock, a descendent of revolutionary patriots, and in the West she had a pioneer spirit important in the mythology of the frontier. She was still wealthy but, like her ideal male contemporary, was generous with her good fortune. She was most noted for charity, and her unselfish, nurturing nature, her love and devotion, made many other human beings happier and healthier. While the ideal woman of 1930 provides evidence of her increased political and social inclusion, perhaps more important for a worried society, she remained a nurturing wife and provided reassurance of a charitable America concerned with the happiness and health of its citizens.

The more than 8,000 obituaries examined for this study provide evidence that the ideal American commemorated in the mass press not only changed with the times but, during each historical era, met some type of social need. In a way, this American provided reassurance about the stability of the dominant culture. In an obituary, this value of a life, which changed over time, brought with it certain responsibilities—sometimes risking life in battle, sometimes laboring in a capitalist system until you dropped dead of a heart attack, and sometimes giving up a public role to maintain domestic harmony. The obituaries that commemorated these lives indeed contributed, in one small way, to the well-being of each era's dominant culture. But these death notices also may have subsumed the individual. On obituary pages of mainstream newspapers, dying in America seemed less about individuality and more about social responsibility. In death, the singular American was portrayed as having an obligation to instruct the living about ideal virtues that would protect national unity and security.

Those Remembered and Forgotten

Of course, the dominant culture became more socially inclusive during these eras of increasing political inclusion, as the newspaper obituaries reflect. Little by little, the percentage of women's obituaries, for example, increased with each new era, and women's attributes changed, including their growing public role and eventual political voice. Still, many people were forgotten, the obituary pages offering an incomplete reflection of American culture. Native Americans, for example, were commemorated in Jacksonian era obituaries only when they were associated with the white culture and provided examples of subjection. In later years, when that particular reassurance appeared unnecessary, this sample indicated that the Native American disappeared from obituary pages in these urban publications. Likewise, African Americans were typically remembered in nineteenth-century obituaries only if they fulfilled some sort of news or cultural value associated with the dominant Caucasian culture. Their numbers inched upward, providing evidence of increased social inclusion, albeit slowly. Mainstream newspapers appeared not to notice the deaths of the vast majority of African Americans. Children, the poor, socially outcast, or disabled Americans also failed to fit a social ideal that would allow them to be part of public memory. If newspaper obituaries were reflectors of a society becoming inclusive, they still had a long way to go to be accurate indicators.

Lessons from the Past

What can modern obituary writers—or readers—learn from these historic American newspaper obituaries? Such writers could become more aware of issues of inclusion on today's obituary pages. An examination of the criteria not only for who is commemorated but also for what kinds of attributes are considered worthy of remembering would likely illuminate some modern social taboos and exclusions. This issue, of course, has been discussed to some degree in the press and in trade publications. Columnist Michael Kinsley of the *New Republic* ruminated on the *New York Times*'s obituary policy, saying, "the criteria for deciding who is included, as well as the hierarchies of placement and size, are deeply mysterious," and suggesting that "parentage" might be the determining factor.[4] But Max Frankel, writing in the *New York Times Magazine*, defended the newspaper's record: "The *Times* assigns obits to good writers, often those with direct knowledge of the person's achievements, and to sensitive editors who aim to balance candor and respect. In their best moments, the obits land on the piquant details that illuminate the lives of even the less-than-famous." But Frankel argues that most newspapers, even serious ones, are not as diligent, despite the fact that readership surveys consistently recognize devotion to the obituary page.[5] One Alabama newspaper provided the exception to that rule. The tiny *Guntersville Advertiser-Gleam* received national recognition for its colorful obituaries. Former editor Porter Harvey told *American Journalism Review* in 1994 that his newspaper does "an obit on everyone."[6] Still other publications have made obituary writing a priority and turned their obituary pages into feature pages. The *New York Herald-Tribune* won a Pulitzer Prize in 1961 for its front-page account of the death of Metropolitan Opera star Leonard Warren.[7] However, most mainstream newspapers either cannot or will not publish an obituary for everyone. They must, because of space limitations, pick and choose. The questions become "Who is covered?" and "Who in modern America does not live up to the ideals or meet the special needs of the dominant culture?"

Modern obituary pages also provide hints to complex social issues concerning the individual death. For example, the *Eugene (Ore.) Register-Guard* prompted a debate when it published a 1995 obituary for an in utero death. Editors later reconsidered the decision and formulated a policy that included obituaries only for stillborn deaths carried to full term.[8] The AIDS epidemic, too, posed questions of confidentiality and privacy regarding the inclusion of cause of death in obituaries, and newspapers adopted different methods for handling these problems. For example, when designer Perry Ellis died, obituaries in the *Washington Post* and *USA Today* mentioned AIDS, though the *New York Times* and the *Los Angeles Times* did not.[9] Why? Are values different in different media units? The obituary pages, in fact, became a battleground when activist groups began asking newspapers to fully report AIDS deaths in an effort to garner support for research and treatment.[10] Again, newspaper obituaries were needed to fulfill a social need, to contribute to a society's well-being. And again, they served not only as a chronicle of death but also as a preserver of the worth of an American life, despite taboo topics.

For historians, the American press provides a valuable resource of a culture. Modern as well as historic newspaper obituaries harbor a wealth of information about a changing, always dynamic American society. Yet they are not perfect primary sources. For example, some obituary decisions might have been made as policy, some because of the competitive nature of the newspaper business, some because of economic constraints that limited space or staff, and some because of simple happenstance. Each of these variables would affect obituary inclusion and the historic death notice's value as a reflector of the worth, collectively, of the singular American life.

Yet taken collectively, obituaries can add to our knowledge about the historical value of a particular American life, a life that truly holds an important place in an egalitarian society. In fact, the value of a singular life is this study's most important finding. In the end, it points to more than just a dominant culture that excludes those without power, and it points to more than a nation that reveals, to varying degrees, its preoccupation with death. This examination of obituaries published during selected political and cultural turning points, eras when America was becoming more politically inclusive, shows that Americans value each other and, indeed, value life for collective reasons. They value a long, robust, and full life, a life that is uniquely American, and a life that ensures social self-preservation. A typical Victorian obituary would carry the statement, "in life we are in the midst of death," but as this study suggests, at least on the obituary pages of historic mainstream American newspapers, in death we are in the midst of life.

Notes

Chapter 1

1. "William P. Custis," *Daily National Intelligencer,* 18 November 1838, 3.

2. Endres, "Frontier Obituaries," 54.

3. Ibid.

4. Kastenbaum, Peyton, and Kastenbaum, "Sex Discrimination," 351.

5. There are many fine discussions of public memory, including the classic work by Halbwachs, *On Collective Memory,* on which many studies are based. This particular definition, a typical example, is from Bodnar, "Public Memory," 76.

6. Allen Baddeley, "The Psychology of Remembering and Forgetting," in *Memory,* ed. Butler, 58.

7. Schwartz, "Social Context," 377.

8. Connerton, *How Societies Remember,* 3.

9. Ibid.

10. Hartman, "Public Memory," 239.

11. Hareven, "Search," 137.

12. Halbwachs, *On Collective Memory,* 83.

13. Amato, "Death," 259.

14. Huyssen, *Twilight Memories,* 3.

15. Lowenthal, "Timeless Past," 1264.
16. Halbwachs, *On Collective Memory*, 175–76.
17. Kammen, *Mystic Chords*, 6.
18. Bodnar, *Remaking America*, 22.
19. Schwartz, "Social Change," 221.
20. Bodnar, *Remaking America*, 26.
21. Kammen, *Mystic Chords*, 688.
22. Boorstin, *The Image*, 3, 5.
23. Ibid., 37.
24. Huyssen, *Twilight Memories*, 4–5.
25. "Michael Quinn," 4.
26. John R. Gillis, "Memory and Identity: The History of a Relationship," in *Commemorations*, ed. Gillis, 3.
27. Bodnar, "Public Memory," 75.
28. Bodnar, *Remaking America*, 48.
29. Ibid., 75.
30. Kammen, *Mystic Chords*, 38.
31. Schudson, *Power*, 37.
32. Warner, *Living and the Dead*, 54–55.
33. Whaley, *Mirrors of Mortality*, 14.
34. Farrell, *Inventing*, 5, 7
35. Wheeler, *Heaven*, 28.
36. Curl, *Victorian Celebration*, 169.
37. Stevenson, *Victorian Homefront*, 143.
38. Ibid.
39. See, for example, Sloane, *Last Great Necessity*; Curl, *Victorian Celebration*; and Barnard, *To Prove*.
40. Farrell, *Inventing*, 221.
41. Ibid., 9, 13.
42. Gitlin, *Whole World*, 2.
43. Ibid., 6.
44. Pan and Kosicki, "Framing Analysis," 55.
45. See, for example, Entman, "Framing U.S. Coverage" and "Framing: Toward Clarification"; Iyengar, *Is Anyone Responsible?*; Tuchman, *Making News*; and Cohen and Wolfsfeld, eds., *Framing*.
46. Drake and Donohue, "Communicative Framing Theory."
47. Norris, ed., *Women*, 6.

Chapter 2

1. Among the many discussions of Jackson's election as a crossroads in American history are Ward, *Andrew Jackson*, and Remini, *Election*. For a discussion of the evolution of political culture during the Civil War era, see Morone, "Struggle," 424–31.

2. Remini, *Andrew Jackson*, 7.

3. Welter, *Mind*, 77.

4. Remini, *Andrew Jackson*, 6.

5. Cunningham, *Popular Images*, 209.

6. Watson, "In Retrospect," 739.

7. For discussions of such resistance to full citizenship, see Rogers, ed., *Voting*.

8. Mott, *History*, 268.

9. Luxon, Niles' Weekly Register, 88.

10. Mott, *American Journalism*, 176.

11. Ames, *History*, vii.

12. William David Sloan, "The Party Press, 1793–1833," in *Media*, ed. Sloan and Startt, 90.

13. Ibid., 93, 115.

14. Ibid., 114.

15. Emery and Emery, *Press*, 117.

16. Ibid., 103; Schudson, *Power*, 33.

17. See William Webster, *High School Pronouncing Dictionary*, 186; or Noah Webster, *Compendious Dictionary*, 205. Barry Schwartz has written about the significance of the "commemoration" in American public memory. He says a commemoration is more than a mere chronicle but is invested with an extraordinary significance in the public's conception of the past ("Social Context," 377).

18. Because the headlines of these eras are so similar, most obituaries are cited in the notes by the deceased's name. In the newspapers, these names were typically published in boldfaced type.

19. "Death of Col. Daniel Boone," *Niles' Weekly Register*, 19 September 1818, 64.

20. "Chronicle," *Niles' Weekly Register*, 7 November 1818, 176; "Col. Boone," *Niles' Weekly Register*, 26 December 1818, 328.

21. "James B. Lane," *National Intelligencer*, 27 August 1818, 3.

22. "Paul Carrington," *National Intelligencer*, 10 July 1818, 3.

23. "Dr. Richard C. Dale," *Niles' Weekly Register*, 23 May 1818, 223.

24. Among the many discussions of early-nineteenth-century women and work are Ryan, *Cradle*, 172–73; and Dublin, *Women*.

25. See, for example, "John Chestnut," *Niles' Weekly Register*, 16 May 1818, 192.

26. See, for example, "Elisa Prior," *Niles' Weekly Register*, 31 January 1818, 277; "Joshua Barney," *Niles' Weekly Register*, 12 December 1818, 265; and "Asa Danforth," *National Intelligencer*, 29 September 1818, 3.

27. "General David Humphries," *Niles' Weekly Register*, 28 February 1818, 15.

28. "Richard Brown," *National Intelligencer*, 14 February 1818, 3.

29. "Benjamin Walker," *National Intelligencer*, 23 January 1818, 3.

30. "Patrick O'Flinn," *Niles' Weekly Register*, 11 July 1818, 344.

31. Bodnar, *Remaking America*, 26.

32. "George Rogers Clark," *National Intelligencer*, 12 March 1818, 3.

33. "Bennet Searcy," *National Intelligencer*, 6 February 1818, 3.

34. See "Longevity," *Niles' Weekly Register*, 28 February 1818, 16; and "Longevity," *National Intelligencer*, 1 February 1818, 3.

35. For examples, see "James Hickey," *National Intelligencer*, 20 July 1818, 3; "Jake Baker," *National Intelligencer*, 17 November 1818, 3; and "Jedediah Huntington," *Niles' Weekly Register*, 17 October 1818, 126.

36. "David Mitchell," *Niles' Weekly Register*, 27 June 1818, 311.

37. "The Late Mrs. Adams," *Niles' Weekly Register*, 14 November 1818, 200; "The Late Madam Adams," *National Intelligencer*, 7 November 1818, 2.

38. See, for example, "Emily Benjamin," *National Intelligencer*, 16 March 1818, 3.

39. "Sarah English," *National Intelligencer*, 22 September 1818, 3.

40. Laderman, *Sacred Remains*, 40.

41. "Eleanor Howard," *Niles' Weekly Register*, 20 June 1818, 256; "Christopher Greenup," *National Intelligencer*, 15 May 1818, 3.

42. "Jake Baker," *National Intelligencer*, 17 November 1818, 3; "David Ross," *National Intelligencer*, 23 June 1818, 3; and "James Carr," *National Intelligencer*, 16 September 1818, 3.

43. "Thomas Ramsey," *National Intelligencer*, 15 September 1818, 3.

44. "Zina Allen Turner," *National Intelligencer*, 16 August 1818, 3.

45. "Ebenezer Little," *National Intelligencer*, 16 August 1818, 3.

46. According to Schudson, "reporting as a specialized journalistic activity did not begin until the 1830s" (*Power*, 95).

47. See "Lieutenant Colonel Armistead," *Niles' Weekly Register*, 9 May 1818, 190–91; "Tribute to the Brave," *Niles' Weekly Register*, 4 July 1818, 822; and "Another Revolutionary Officer Gone," *Niles' Weekly Register*, 17 October 1818, 126.

48. "Lieutenant Colonel Armistead," *Niles' Weekly Register*, 9 May 1818, 190.

49. "Rebecca Lowe," *National Intelligencer*, 27 January 1818, 3.

50. See, as examples, "Sally Maria Cook," *National Intelligencer*, 14 December 1818, 3; "Paul Carrington," *National Intelligencer*, 10 July 1818, 3; "William Goddard," *National Intelligencer*, 2 January 1818, 3.

51. "Jedediah Huntington," *Niles' Weekly Register*, 17 October 1818, 126.

52. "William P. Custis," *Daily National Intelligencer*, 18 November 1838, 3.

53. "Lorenzo Daponte," *Niles' National Register*, 25 August 1838, 403.

54. "Jane Maria Bury," *Daily National Intelligencer*, 29 June 1838, 3.

55. "Sister Mary Bernardine," *Daily National Intelligencer*, 17 June 1838, 3; "Sister Francis Furry," *Daily National Intelligencer*, 10 January 1838, 3.

56. "Joshua Humphreys," *Daily National Intelligencer*, 6 February 1838, 3.

57. "Dr. John B. Tilden," *Daily National Intelligencer*, 8 August 1838, 3.

58. "Thomas Bradford," *Daily National Intelligencer*, 13 May 1838, 3.

59. "Charles Gatliff," *Niles' National Register*, 4 August 1838, 36.

60. "Death of Gen. Clark," *Niles' National Register*, 15 September 1838, 34.

61. "Alexander Milne," *Niles' National Register*, 10 November 1838, 163.

62. Farrell, *Inventing*, 5.

63. "William P. Custis," *Daily National Intelligencer*, 18 November 1838, 3.

64. "Catharine Dent," *Daily National Intelligencer*, 29 September 1838, 3.

65. See "William E. Payne," *Niles' National Register*, 18 August 1838, 400.

66. "George Small," *Daily National Intelligencer*, 7 September 1838, 3; "Daniel Clarke," *Daily National Intelligencer*, 30 December 1838, 3; "Reuben Conway," *Daily National Intelligencer*, 11 January 1838, 3. See also "Isaac McKin," *Niles' National Register*, 7 April 1838, 1; "Robert C. Jennings," *Daily National Intelligencer*, 8 November 1838, 3; and "William Patterson," *Niles' National Register*, 25 August 1838, 401.

67. "Mary Vincent," *Daily National Intelligencer*, 5 May 1838, 3.

68. "Mary Rose," *Daily National Intelligencer*, 8 July 1838, 3.

69. "Emeline Elizabeth Morgan," *Daily National Intelligencer*, 8 October 1838, 3.

70. "Mingo Mushulatubbee," *Daily National Intelligencer*, 10 October 1838, 3.

71. For examples, see "Washington Joseph Ward," *Daily National Intelligencer*, 4 September 1838, 3; and "Mary Berry Williams," *Daily National Intelligencer*, 1 May 1838, 3.

72. "Maria Angelina Devlin," *Daily National Intelligencer*, 1 October 1838, 3; "William Wirt Goldsborough," *Daily National Intelligencer*, 16 December 1838, 3.

73. For a discussion of medical practices from that era, see Bynum, *Science*.

74. "Henry Melville," *Niles' National Register*, 14 April 1838, 112; "A Child's Affection for a Kitten," *Niles' National Register*, 22 September 1838, 64; "Thomas Barclay," *Daily National Intelligencer*, 4 February 1838, 3.

75. "Nicholas Stonestreet," *Daily National Intelligencer*, 30 December 1838, 3.

76. "Mary Rose," *Daily National Intelligencer*, 8 July 1838, 3.

77. "Elizabeth Buchanan," *Daily National Intelligencer*, 29 March 1838, 3.

78. "Eleanor Sprigg," *Daily National Intelligencer*, 20 September 1838, 3.

79. "Mary Berry," *Daily National Intelligencer*, 1 May 1838, 3.

80. "Daniel Clark," *Daily National Intelligencer*, 30 December 1838, 3.

81. "Margaret M. Marache," *Daily National Intelligencer*, 16 February 1838, 3; and "Ann Newman Balch," *Daily National Intelligencer*, 10 October 1838, 3.

82. "General William Colfax," *Niles' National Register*, 22 September 1838, 64; "James B. Thornton," *Niles' National Register*, 19 May 1838, 78; "Timothy J. Carter," *Niles' National Register*, 24 March 1838, 1; "The Funeral of the Late Commodore John Rodgers," *Niles' National Register*, 11 August 1838, 3.

83. "General David Humphries," *Niles' Weekly Register*, 28 February 1818, 15.

84. See "Dr. John B. Tilden," *Daily National Intelligencer*, 8 August 1838, 3; and "Death of Gen. Clark," *Niles' National Register*, 15 September 1838, 34.

85. "Mary Rose," *Daily National Intelligencer*, 8 July 1838, 3.

86. "Eleanore Sprigg," *Daily National Intelligencer*, 20 September 1838, 3.

87. Amato, "Death," 259.

Chapter 3

1. However, the status of the individual versus community in American culture has always been in flux, shaped in part by the struggle and assimilation of immigrants. For a discussion of the evolution of political culture during the Civil War era, see Morone, "Struggle," 424–31.

2. Donald W. Rogers, "Introduction—The Right to Vote in American History," in *Voting*, ed. Rogers, 10.

3. Ibid., 11.

4. Kammen, *Mystic Chords*, 13.

5. Laderman, *Sacred Remains*, 8, 9.

6. Ibid., 22.

7. Ibid., 53.

8. Ibid., 136–37.

9. See the discussion of medical science in the United States in Bynum, *Science*, 114–17.

10. Elazar, *Building*, 127.

11. Mott, *American Journalism*, 279–80.

12. Ibid., 249; Dabney, *One Hundred Great Years*, 83.

13. Dabney, *One Hundred Great Years*, 104–5.

14. Emery and Emery, *Press*, 123.

15. Ibid., 360.

16. The *Baltimore Sun* occasionally published on its front page an advertising-rate box that indicated that the newspaper charged twenty-five cents for funeral notices and regular advertising rates for "extra" obituary notices published near the death notices column ("Cash Terms of Advertising," *Baltimore Sun*, 24 August 1855, 1). There is no evidence that the newspaper charged for news obituaries. Though the *New York Daily Times* and the *New Orleans Picayune* did not run information about advertising rates during the sample weeks, the similarities in the format of the three newspapers' obituary notices indicates that these two papers may have had similar policies.

17. "The Character of Malcom Clark," *New York Daily Times*, 4 June 1855, 2.

18. "Death of an Eminent Statistician," *New York Daily Times*, 2 June 1855, 2.

19. "Death of a Veteran—Conrad Bush," *New York Daily Times*, 5 January 1855, 5.

20. "The Last of the Heroes of Bennington Gone," *New York Daily Times*, 3 February 1855, 3.

21. "Peter Van Antwerp," *New York Daily Times*, 3 April 1855, 5; "Death of Major Paulding's Widow," *New York Daily Times*, 7 November 1855, 5.

22. "Recent Deaths: Jonathan Gillett," *New York Daily Times*, 2 April 1855, 3.

23. "Recent Deaths: Abraham Hilliard," *New York Daily Times*, 5 March 1855, 5.

24. "Death of a Monomaniac," *New York Daily Times*, 3 August 1855, 5.

25. "Mary Clark," *New York Daily Times*, 1 August 1855, 8; "Mary Cass," *New York Daily Times*, 3 April 1855, 8; "Catharine King," *New York Daily Times*, 5 September 1855, 8.

26. Tocqueville, *Democracy*, 114.

27. "A Colored Man Fell Dead," *New York Daily Times*, 4 May 1855, 1.

28. "Death from Burns," *New York Daily Times*, 7 May 1855, 3.

29. "Jane Sophia Tappan Cornish," *New York Daily Times*, 7 March 1855, 8.

30. "Jeanie Hall," *New York Daily Times*, 3 January 1855, 8.

31. "John Henry Van Sant," *New York Daily Times*, 6 August 1855, 8.

32. "Mary Cass," *New York Daily Times*, 3 April 1855, 8.

33. "Death of an Aged Clergyman," *New Orleans Picayune*, 1 December 1855, 2.

34. "Another of the Soldiers of the Revolution Gone," *New Orleans Picayune*, 4 December 1855, 1.

35. "Death of a Venerable Lady," *New Orleans Picayune*, 7 July 1855, 1.

36. "Obituary of Francis T. Porter," *New Orleans Picayune*, 1 March 1855, 2.

37. "Longevity," *New Orleans Picayune*, 3 October 1855, 2.

38. "Buffalo Chief," *New Orleans Picayune*, 5 October 1855, 2.

39. "Death of an Actor," *New Orleans Picayune*, 3 January 1855, 2.

40. "Death of Dr. John C. Calhoun," *New Orleans Picayune*, 6 August 1855, 1. For a discussion of the yellow fever epidemic, see Duffy, *Sword*.

41. "Augustus A. Soria," *New Orleans Picayune*, 6 April 1855, 2; "Death of Doesticks," *New Orleans Picayune*, 7 June 1855, 1.

42. For a discussion of religion in both regions during this era, see Rose, *Victorian America*, 17–67.

43. "The Late James M. Oldham," *New Orleans Picayune*, 4 August 1855, 2; "Sallie Cummings," *New Orleans Picayune*, 4 July 1855, 2; "Obituary," *New Orleans Picayune*, 4 August 1855, 1; "John S. Barrow," *New Orleans Picayune*, 1 September 1855, 1.

44. "Obituary: Laura Grace Hyatt," *New Orleans Picayune*, 4 June 1855, 2.

45. "The Funeral of Francis T. Porter," *New Orleans Picayune*, 2 March 1855, 2.

46. "Death of an Octogenarian," *Baltimore Sun*, 1 March 1855, 1.

47. "The Death of Mrs. Taney," *Baltimore Sun*, 4 October 1855, 1.

48. "Henry Gassett," *Baltimore Sun*, 2 August 1855, 4.

49. "Death of Mrs. Captain Reed," *Baltimore Sun*, 3 August 1855, 4.

50. "Death of a Slave in Syracuse," *Baltimore Sun*, 2 April 1855, 1.

51. "Death of Bishop Capers, of the M.E. Church, South," *Baltimore Sun*, 3 February 1855, 1.

52. "Death of a Literary Lady," *Baltimore Sun*, 4 December 1855, 1.

53. "Death of Young Ellis," *Baltimore Sun*, 2 August 1855, 1; "William Ainscow," *Baltimore Sun*, 1 August 1855, 4; "Mrs. John Hevener, " *Baltimore Sun*, 1 August 1855, 4; "Singular Cause of Death," *Baltimore Sun*, 2 October 1855, 4; "Death of an Old Printer," *Baltimore Sun*, 2 May 1855, 1; "Francis M. McKnight," *Baltimore Sun*, 6 July 1855, 2; "T. Charles Ringgold,"

Baltimore Sun, 3 May 1855, 2; "Lieutenant Heth," *Baltimore Sun*, 4 October 1855, 2.

54. "Sudden Death," *Baltimore Sun*, 6 June 1855, 1.

55. "Singular Presentiment of Death," *Baltimore Sun*, 5 February 1855, 1.

56. "Burial of a Singular Character," *Baltimore Sun*, 6 February 1855, 1.

57. "Harriet McLain," *Baltimore Sun*, 5 February 1855, 2.

58. "John Walker," *Baltimore Sun*, 1 May 1855, 2.

59. Emery and Emery, *Press*, 360.

60. Thomas Foster, as his obituary noted, "calmly resigned his soul into the hands of his Maker on Sunday evening, just as the church bells were ringing for public worship. The venerable man was sitting in the midst of his family, conversing affectionately and cheerfully, when he suddenly fell from his chair, and his happy spirit had taken its flight" ("Death of a Veteran," *New York Times*, 7 October 1870, 1).

61. "Obituary: Major-General Joseph E. Hamblin," *New York Times*, 5 July 1870, 3.

62. "Obituary: General Hiram Walbridge," *New York Times*, 7 December 1870, 1.

63. See *New York Times*, 1–7 April 1870.

64. See "The Late Alphens Chapin of Boston," *New York Times*, 6 March 1870, 2; and "Daniel Delevan," *New York Times*, 2 April 1870, 8.

65. "Samuel Campbell," *New York Times*, 1 December 1870, 5.

66. "Daniel B. Fearing," *New York Times*, 1 December 1870, 2; "General Hiram Walbridge," *New York Times*, 7 December 1870, 1.

67. "Death of Dr. Gunning M. Bedford Yesterday Morning—Interesting Sketch of His Life," *New York Times*, 6 September 1870, 2.

68. "Obituary: John McGrath," *New York Times*, 5 December 1870, 3.

69. "Death of Dr. Charlotte Lozier," *New York Times*, 4 January 1870, 5; "Funeral of Mrs. Dr. Lozier," *New York Times*, 6 January 1870, 5.

70. "Burial of a Naval Hero," *New York Times*, 4 August 1870, 3.

71. See, for example, obituaries in *New York Times* on 5 February, 2 and 4 August 1870.

72. "Charles Rufus Adams," *New Orleans Picayune*, 2 December 1870, 1.

73. "Death of Col. D. Beltzhoover," *New Orleans Picayune*, 3 November 1870, 2.

74. "Jules G. Oliver," *New Orleans Picayune*, 6 April 1870, 4.

75. "Mark Walton," *New Orleans Picayune*, 4 December 1870, 1.

76. "An Old Officer Gone," *New Orleans Picayune*, 6 February 1870, 2.

77. "Death of Ross, the Cherokee Chief," *New Orleans Picayune*, 1 April 1870, 10.

78. "Hannah Florence," *New Orleans Picayune*, 3 August 1870, 4.

79. "Death of Anna Cora Mowatt Ritchie," *Baltimore Sun*, 1 August 1870, 2.

80. "Death of Col. C. T. Ames," *New Orleans Picayune*, 6 November 1870, 1; "John D. Nicholson," *New Orleans Picayune*, 3 December 1870, 4; "Joseph De Hamel," *New Orleans Picayune*, 2 February 1870, 6.

81. "Governor Henry Allen," *New Orleans Picayune*, 21 November 1870, 1.

82. The advertising rates for advertising obituary notices was the same in 1855 and in 1870. For an example of those rates, see "Cash Rates of Advertising," *Baltimore Sun*, 7 July 1870, 1.

83. "The Funeral of Admiral Farragut," *Baltimore Sun*, 1 October 1870, 1.

84. "Death of Coleman Yellott," *Baltimore Sun*, 1 August 1870, 4.

85. "Death of a Southern Planter," *Baltimore Sun*, 5 October 1870, 2.

86. "A Wealthy Colored Woman," *Baltimore Sun*, 4 January 1870, 4.

87. "Death of an Aged Colored Woman," *Baltimore Sun*, 1 April 1870, 4.

88. "A Centenarian Gone," *Baltimore Sun*, 5 December 1870, 3.

89. "Death of a Prominent Colored Politician," *Baltimore Sun*, 2 September 1870, 1.

90. "Henry Bates," *Baltimore Sun*, 4 April 1870, 2.

91. "Death of a Venerable Matron," *Baltimore Sun*, 1 September 1870, 4.

92. "Death of Anna Cora Mowatt Ritchie," *Baltimore Sun*, 1 August 1870, 2.

93. "Death of a Well Known 'Doctress,'" *Baltimore Sun*, 5 January 1870, 4.

94. "Nellie A. Herold," *Baltimore Sun*, 2 July 1870, 2. See also "Sarah Craig," *Baltimore Sun*, 7 July 1870, 2; and "Lenox B. Lewis," *Baltimore Sun*, 6 October 1870, 2.

Chapter 4

1. For discussions of these turn-of-the-century changes, see Lears, "Roots of Antimodernism: The Crisis of Cultural Authority during the Late Nineteenth Century," in his *No Place*, 4–58; Susman, "Personality and the Making of Twentieth-Century Culture," in his *Culture*, 271–85; and Seymour Martin Lipset, "A Changing American Character," in *Distorted Image*, ed. Hartshorne, 302–30.

2. For a discussion of the suffrage movement in the late nineteenth century, see Ellen Carol DuBois, "Taking Law into Their Own Hands: Voting Women during Reconstruction," in *Voting*, ed. Rogers, 67–81.

3. Some scholars believe that the women's movement disintegrated during the 1920s because of apathy, but others argue that the decade's focus on association and community strengthened the movement. See Alpern and Baum, "Female Ballots"; Lemons, *Woman Citizen;* and Schlozman et al., "Gender."

4. Mott, *American Journalism*, 654.

5. Ibid., 562, 584.

6. Ibid., 473–75.

7. There were 2,200 English language dailies and 14,000 weeklies in 1910 (Beasley, "Emergence," 344).

8. Mott, *American Journalism*, 347–54.

9. George Everett, "The Age of New Journalism," in *Media*, ed. Sloan and Startt, 290–91.

10. Ross, *Writing*, 130.

11. The funeral industry gained in strength at the turn of the century. The National Funeral Directors Association formed in 1883 and focused during its formative years on ethics, social responsibility, and new innovations in the field (Laderman, *Sacred Remains*, 168–69).

12. Maulsby, *Getting*, 254, 257, 256, 259, 255.

13. Porter and Luxon, *Reporter*, 190–91.

14. MacDougall, *College Course*, 288–89, 299, 292.

15. Lears, *No Place*, 54–55.

16. Amato, "Death," 259.

17. For a discussion of early-twentieth-century America's consumer orientation, see Potter, *People*, 173–75.

18. Lears, *No Place*, 302–3.

19. Susman, "Personality and the Making of Twentieth-Century Culture," in his *Culture*, 271–85.

20. Katzenstein, "Constitutional Politics," 86–87.

21. Lears, *No Place*, 304–5.

22. Katzenstein, "Constitutional Politics," 87–88, 92.

23. "Elizabeth Inez McCarty Schack," *New York Times*, 7 March 1910, 9.

24. "Mrs. A. E. Plant Killed," *New York Times*, 5 September 1910, 1.

25. "Edith Walsh Marshall," *New York Times*, 6 February 1910, 11.

26. "Mrs. Pierre L. Ronalds Dead," *New York Times*, 4 June 1910, 9.

27. "Cashmere Shawl Lady Dead," *New York Times*, 7 February 1910, 9.

28. "Mrs. Flora Darling Dead," *New York Times*, 7 January 1910, 9.

29. "Eliza Haverly," *New York Times*, 5 July 1910, 13.

30. "Wealthy Woman Hermit Found Dead," *New York Times*, 6 December 1910, 13.

31. "Emily Briggs," *New York Times*, 5 July 1910, 13.

32. "Myra Kelly, Writer of Child Life, Dead," *New York Times*, 1 April 1910, 11.

33. "Mrs. Eddy Dies of Pneumonia; No Doctor Near," *New York Times*, 5 December 1910, 1.

34. "Anna M. Hammer," *New York Times*, 1 May 1910, 11.

35. "Augusta Cooper Bristol," *New York Times*, 6 October 1910, 11.

36. See the *Chicago Tribune*'s special section on the death of Mary Baker Eddy, 5 December 1910.

37. "Life of Founder of Christian Science," *San Francisco Chronicle*, 5 December 1910, 2.

38. "Pioneer Woman Passes Away in Berkeley," *San Francisco Chronicle*, 4 July 1910, 4; "Death's Hand Falls on a Pioneer Woman," *San Francisco Chronicle*, 1 May 1910, 37.

39. "Widow of Prominent Pioneer Is Dead," *San Francisco Chronicle*, 7 July 1910, 2.

40. "Pioneer Woman Dies Past Century Mark," *San Francisco Chronicle*, 6 November 1910, 40.

41. "Mary McKnight," *Chicago Tribune*, 7 July 1910, 3; "Harriet Marshall," *Chicago Tribune*, 2 December 1910, 16.

42. "Chicago Woman Dead at 101," *Chicago Tribune*, 7 June 1910, 3.

43. For discussions of some of these events and symbols, see Kammen, *Mystic Chords*; and Bodnar, *Remaking America*.

44. "Founder of D.A.R. is Dead," *Chicago Tribune*, 7 January 1910, 3.

45. "Gen. Streight's Widow Dies," *Chicago Tribune*, 6 June 1910, 4.

46. "Chicago Woman Dead at 101," *Chicago Tribune*, 7 June 1910, 3. As discussed in chapter 1, generational memory ties family history with national history by linking individual citizens with specific historic moments (Hareven, "Search," 137).

47. "Michael O'Rourke," *New York Times*, 4 March 1910, 9.

48. "Captain Joshua W. Crosby," *New York Times*, 7 April 1910, 11.

49. "Samuel S. Sanford Dead," *New York Times*, 7 January 1910, 9.

50. "William H. Class," *New York Times*, 6 January 1910, 9.

51. "Memorial to J. E. Simmons," *New York Times*, 7 October 1910, 11.

52. See, as examples, "Alanson A. Sumner Dead," *New York Times*, 4 December 1910, 13; "Robert H. Shearer," *New York Times*, 3 February 1910, 9; "Lived as a Hermit amid City's Rush," *New York Times*, 1 August 1910, 7; "Minneapolis's Richest Man Dead," *New York Times*, 4 May 1910, 11; and "Frank L. Blaisdell," *New York Times*, 7 January 1910, 9.

53. "John S. Huyler Dies in 65th Year," *New York Times*, 2 October 1910, 13.

54. See, as examples,"Pioneer Is Called," *San Francisco Chronicle*, 3 December 1910, 4; "Pioneer of Fifties Dies at Stockton," *San Francisco Chronicle*, 1 May 1910, 42; and "D. C. Breed, Pioneer, Is Dead at Oakland," *San Francisco Chronicle*, 1 May 1910, 36; "Death Overtakes Pioneer Clothier," *San Francisco Chronicle*, 6 February 1910, 58; "Calvin Ewing Is Called by Death," *San Francisco Chronicle*, 6 February 1910, 40; "Pioneer Passes Away After Notable Career," *San Francisco Chronicle*, 2 July 1910, 21.

55. "Sheriff of Early Days Dies at Advanced Age," *San Francisco Chronicle*, 1 September 1910, 3.

56. "Pioneer Settler of Hayward Dies," *San Francisco Chronicle*, 4 February 1910, 8.

57. "Henry S. Aldrich," *Chicago Tribune*, 5 January 1910, 3.

58. "Justice Fuller Closes Busy Life," *Chicago Tribune*, 5 July 1910, 9.

59. "T. C. Platt Dead; End Unexpected," *Chicago Tribune*, 7 March 1910, 1.

60. "Brilliant, but Errs; Dies," *Chicago Tribune*, 1 January 1910, 2.

61. "D. C. Breed, Pioneer, Is Dead in Oakland," *San Francisco Chronicle*, 1 May 1910, 36; "Pioneer Passes Away after Notable Career," *San Francisco Chronicle*, 2 July 1910, 21.

62. "'Forty-Niner' Who Dies at Age of 84," *Chicago Tribune*, 5 June 1910, 6; "John Henderson," *Chicago Tribune*, 7 May 1910, 5; "Saw Lincoln Slain; Is Dead," *Chicago Tribune*, 4 January 1910, 4.

63. "Lincoln Funeral Aid Dies," *Chicago Tribune*, 2 December 1910, 8.

64. "Gordon Davis," *New York Times*, 3 March 1910, 9.

65. "Ex-Congressman John M. Atwater," *New York Times*, 6 July 1910, 7; "John Monroe Reuck," *New York Times*, 3 March 1910, 9.

66. "Dies in a Dance at Sea," *New York Times*, 1 April 1910, 7.

67. "Pioneer Chicago Showman Is Dead," *Chicago Tribune*, 7 October 1910, 9.

68. "Broward Dies under Knife," *New York Times*, 2 October 1910, 13.

69. "Pioneer Settler of Hayward Dies," *San Francisco Chronicle*, 4 February 1910, 8.

70. "Frederick Zeile Called by Death" and "Former Bank President and Park Commissioner Succumbs to Operation," *San Francisco Chronicle*, 4 December 1910, 31.

71. "Ex-Minister Edwin H. Terrell," *New York Times*, 3 July 1910, 7.

72. "Commits Suicide by Hanging," *San Francisco Chronicle*, 5 March 1910, 9.

73. "John G. Carlisle, 75, Dies in Hotel Home," *New York Times*, 1 August 1910, 7.

74. See, as examples, "Tommy McCarthy Is Laid at Rest," *San Francisco Chronicle*, 3 May 1910, 5; and "Last Services for Rev. George G. Adams," *San Francisco Chronicle*, 7 September 1910, 9.

75. "Mary L. Keating," *New York Times*, 7 December 1930, 31; "Julia T. Montague," *New York Times*, 7 October 1930, 29; and "Dr. E. Alberta Read Dies," *New York Times*, 3 September 1930, 27.

76. "Mrs. Robert Rankin," *New York Times*, 6 November 1930, 27.

77. "Mother Jones Dies; Led Mine Workers," *New York Times*, 1 December 1930, 23.

78. "Sister Mary Bernard," *New York Times*, 7 August 1930, 21; "Dr. Elizabeth L. Peck Dies in Philadelphia," *New York Times*, 1 October 1930, 29.

79. "Agnes Randolph, Jefferson Kin, Dies," *New York Times*, 5 December 1930, 27.

80. "Mrs. John Blair Dies of Pneumonia," *New York Times*, 6 November 1930, 27.

81. "Mrs. Aaron Schloss," *New York Times*, 1 January 1930, 29.

82. "Elizabeth Clark Dies as She Ends Address," *New York Times*, 5 June 1930, 27; "Dr. Sarah Kendall," *New York Times*, 7 February 1930, 21; "Fannie Bixby Spencer," *New York Times*, 1 April 1930, 32.

83. "Dies at Age of 109," *New York Times*, 4 August 1930, 15.

84. "Mrs. Hugh Hamilton," *New York Times*, 2 December 1930, 27; "Mrs. Lydia Y. Titus, Actress, Is Dead," *New York Times*, 1 January 1930, 29; "Sarah Elvira Colton," *New York Times*, 5 October 1930, 8N; and "Mrs. A. Naumburg, Philanthropist, Dies," *New York Times*, 7 March 1930, 23.

85. "Mrs. Straus Buried; Her Life Eulogized," *New York Times*, 5 May 1930, 23.

86. See, as examples, "Pioneer Mills Graduate Dead," *San Francisco Chronicle*, 4 March 1930, 4–East Bay; "Miss Skinner of Pioneer Family Is Dead at 81," *Chicago Tribune*, 6 November 1930, 35; and "Mrs. Mary Jane Keirl, 72, Lake County Pioneer, Dead," *Chicago Tribune*, 6 April 1930, 16.

87. See, as examples, "Mrs. Hickman Rites Today," *San Francisco Chronicle*, 5 March 1930, 5-C; and "Mrs. M. E. Ackley, Pioneer, Dead at 88," *San Francisco Chronicle*, 4 November 1930, 10.

88. "Mrs. M. E. Cabell of Old Virginia Family Is Dead," *Chicago Tribune*, 6 July 1930, 9.

89. "Agnes Randolph, Jefferson Kin, Dies," *New York Times*, 5 December 1930, 27; "Lizzie Offult Haldeman," *New York Times*, 4 September 1930, 23.

90. Though the depression might have contributed to this phenomenon, many men commemorated in obituaries were elderly, another probable reason for retirements.

91. "W. H. Alford Dies, a Nash Executive," *New York Times*, 5 February 1930, 23.

92. "G. C. Jenkins Dead; Financier Was 94," *New York Times*, 6 June 1930, 25; W. A. M'Gonagle, Railroad Head, Dies," *New York Times*, 3 August 1930, 23.

93. "Tobin, Idol of Needy on Bowery, Is Dead," *New York Times*, 3 December 1930, 27; "Foster Father of 35 Children Dies," *New York Times*, 7 May 1930, 27.

94. "E. H. Litchfield Dies; Realty Operator," *New York Times*, 4 March 1930, 27; "Henry C. Carlson," *New York Times*, 4 October 1930, 17.

95. "A. Y. Baker, Texas Sheriff," *New York Times*, 2 November 1930, 8N.

96. "Creator of Stringless Bean Dies," *New York Times*, 1 November 1930, 21; "John Pond, Editor, Dies," *New York Times*, 2 June 1930, 23; "James V. Hulse Dies," *New York Times*, 5 April 1930, 19.

97. "George O. Page, Inventor, Dies," *New York Times*, 6 April 1930, 30.

98. "A. L. Riker Dead; Motor Car Pioneer," *New York Times*, 2 June 1930, 23; "W. H. Kelly Dies at 66; Inventor of Amalgam," *New York Times*, 7 June 1930, 19.

99. "Rev. Dr. W. D. Cook Dies," *New York Times*, 6 July 1930, 21; "Rufus Lewis Perry Dies," *New York Times*, 7 June 1930, 19; "Edward H. Wright," *New York Times*, 7 August 1930, 21.

100. "Simeon Brucker, Veteran of '61, Taken by Death," *Chicago Tribune*, 2 July 1930, 16; "W. S. Fitch, Indian Fighter, Dies," *New York Times*, 2 May 1930, 23; "W. H. Tisdale Dies," *New York Times*, 7 January 1930, 33; "W. T. Shepherd, Veteran of '61, Is Dead at 88," *Chicago Tribune*, 4 September 1930, 14; "Thomas Terwilliger Sr.," *New York Times*, 2 February 1930, 26; "Henry R. Howland, Philosopher, Dead," *New York Times*, 5 February 1930, 23; "John B. Solley," *New York Times*, 3 September 1930, 27.

101. "Rites Tomorrow for Man Who Saw Lincoln Slain," *Chicago Tribune*, 1 May 1930, 43; "Witness of Lincoln Tragedy Dies," *New York Times*, 5 August 1930, 23; "Emanuel Oberndorfer," *New York Times*, 1 April 1930, 31.

102. See "Deadwood Dick, Western Hero, Indian Fighter, Dead," *San Francisco Chronicle*, 6 May 1930, 3.

103. See "J. M. Hillman's Aged Mother Dies," *San Francisco Chronicle*, 6 August 1930, 3.

104. See, as examples, headlines over photographs of a lawyer and businessman in the *Chronicle* that read "Career Ended" and "Career Closed": "Ralph Ellis, Lawyer, Dead in Berkeley," *San Francisco Chronicle*, 4 September 1930, 3; and "Guy H. Chick Rites Today," *San Francisco Chronicle*, 5 May 1930, 3.

105. "Death Ends Career of Stock 'Junkman,'" *New York Times*, 3 April 1930, 31; "Boy Croesus Dead at 17," *San Francisco Chronicle*, 5 February 1930, 7.

106. Some African Americans were identified by race, but it is difficult to determine whether other obituaries commemorated African Americans without mentioning their race.

Chapter 5

1. Aristotle, *Nicomachean Ethics*, 33.
2. "Sudden Death," *Baltimore Sun*, 7 May 1855, 1.
3. In explaining how a society remembers, Schwartz argues that a commemoration, because it "celebrates and safeguards the ideal," deserves a "qualitatively distinct place in our conception of the past" ("Social Context," 377).
4. Davidson, *Revolution*, 3.
5. Aristotle, *Nicomachean Ethics*, 11.
6. Ibid., 55.
7. Ibid., 53.
8. Ibid., 41.
9. Ibid., 42.
10. Foucault, *Power/Knowledge*, 83.
11. This Foucault quote is part of a discussion of relations of power in Lamb, "Freedom," 451.
12. Foucault, *Discipline and Punish*, 194, discussed in Wilson, "Foucault."
13. Wilson, "Foucault," 170.
14. Foucault, "Madness," 291.
15. For a discussion of this concept, see Noiriel, "Foucault," 560.
16. "Death of Osceola," *Niles' National Register*, 17 February 1838, 387.
17. "Mingo Mushulatubbee," *Daily National Intelligencer*, 10 October 1838, 3.
18. Aristotle, *Nicomachean Ethics*, 144–45.
19. "Death of Mrs. Mills," *Baltimore Sun*, 4 October 1855, 1.
20. Newspapers examined for this study typically identified by race any non-Caucasian person mentioned in either a news article or an obituary, and though it would be difficult to know for sure the race of each person mentioned, this news convention indicates the sparse numbers of people of color.
21. See, for example, "Jane Loane," *Baltimore Sun*, 4 January 1870, 4;

"Longevity," *New Orleans Picayune*, 6 March 1855, 2; and "Longevity," *New Orleans Picayune*, 1 August 1855, 1.

22. Aristotle, *Nicomachean Ethics*, 194, 92.

23. "Death of an Old Servant," *Baltimore Sun*, 3 November 1855, 1; "A Centenarian Gone," *Baltimore Sun*, 5 December 1870, 3.

24. "A Wealthy Colored Woman," *Baltimore Sun*, 4 January 1870, 4.

25. Connerton, *How Societies Remember*, 3.

26. "Mary Ross," *New York Times*, 1 October 1910, 11.

27. See, as an example, "Hannah Florence," *New Orleans Picayune*, 3 August 1870, 4, who was remembered for being "courteous to her equals" and "most kind to the lowly."

28. Aristotle, *Nicomachean Ethics*, 108.

29. "Rev. Cummings, Jail Chaplain, Is Dead at 77," *Chicago Tribune*, 7 November 1930, 36.

30. Obituaries for children were likely to include sentimental poetry and religious imagery rather than attributes of the deceased.

31. Laderman, *Sacred Remains*, 24–25.

32. Ibid., 173.

33. Aristotle, *Nicomachean Ethics*, 92.

34. Foucault, *Discipline and Punish*, 194, discussed in Wilson, "Foucault."

35. "Chicago Woman Dead at 101," *Chicago Tribune*, 7 June 1910, 3.

36. Hartman, "Public Memory," 239.

37. "The Late Judge Knickerbacker," *New York Daily Times*, 5 February 1855, 2.

38. See Aristotle, *Nicomachean Ethics*, 90, 106–41.

39. Ibid., 106–41.

40. "The Late Mrs. Eliza Vredenburgh Porter," *New York Times*, 7 May 1870, 3.

41. "William P. Custis," *Daily National Intelligencer*, 18 November 1838, 3.

42. "Joshua Humphreys," *Daily National Intelligencer*, 6 February 1839, 3.

43. Because affiliations were not as often mentioned in the Jacksonian era, it is difficult to determine whether obituaries were published for Jewish citizens.

44. Aristotle, *Nicomachean Ethics*, 282.

45. "The Death of Prof. Keany by Accident," *Baltimore Sun*, 1 September 1870, 1.

46. "Sudden Death of Senator Platt," *San Francisco Chronicle*, 7 March 1910, 2.

47. "Death Takes Former Wife of F. L. Wright," *San Francisco Chronicle*, 4 January 1930, 17.

48. "Rev. Dr. Elliott, 79, Is Dead in Flint," *New York Times*, 4 November 1930, 27.

49. "Longevity," *New Orleans Picayune*, 3 October 1855, 2.

50. "A Centenarian Gone," *Baltimore Sun*, 4 September 1855, 4.

51. "Dies at the Age of 106," *New York Times*, 3 December 1910, 1.

52. In the early Jacksonian era, an obituary was more likely to list the cause of death as a "lingering illness" or a "short, painful illness."

53. For a discussion of this phenomenon, see Laderman, *Sacred Remains*, 136–37.

54. Lane, *Violent Death*, 60; Hollinger, *Violent Deaths*, 211. Lane has studied incidences of murder, accident, and suicide in nineteenth-century Philadelphia and offers this statistic, which is likely comparable to other cities of considerable size.

55. "James E. Crane Is Called by Death," *San Francisco Chronicle*, 7 May 1910, 8.

56. "Hotel Man Declared Victim of Apoplexy," *San Francisco Chronicle*, 6 February 1930, 8.

57. Lane, *Violent Death*, 15.

58. "Singular Suicide," *Baltimore Sun*, 20 August 1855, 4; "Death by Suicide," *Baltimore Sun*, 2 June 1870, 1.

59. Hollinger, *Violent Deaths*, 209.

60. See, as examples, "B. C. Andrews a Suicide" and "Bank Clerk, Ill, a Suicide," *New York Times*, 1 May 1910, 3; "Commits Suicide by Hanging," *San Francisco Chronicle*, 5 March 1910; "Mrs. John DeSousa," *New York Times*, 1 February 1910, 4.

61. "Aged Berkeley Man Hangs Self in Home," *San Francisco Chronicle*, 4 March 1930, 4.

62. "Dies in Hospital Plunge," *New York Times*, 3 April 1930, 29.

63. "Mrs. Crocker a Suicide," *New York Times*, 3 November 1930, 11.

64. See "Tuohy, Irish Artist, Found Dead in Home," *New York Times*, 4 September 1930, 23; and "P. J. Tuohey [sic] to Be Buried in Ireland," *New York Times*, 6 September 1930, 15.

65. Aristotle, *Nicomachean Ethics*, 181, 183.

66. "Richard Brown," *National Intelligencer*, 14 February 1818, 3.

67. "The Funeral of Mr. Nathan," *New York Times*, 2 August 1870, 1.

68. "Asked to Be Buried at Sea," *New York Times*, 3 July 1910, 7.

69. "Daughter to Burn Body of Noted Free Thinker," *San Francisco Chronicle*, 5 February 1910, 2.

Chapter 6

1. "William P. Custis," *Daily National Intelligencer,* 18 November 1838, 3.
2. For information about the Associated Press, see Beasley, "Emergence," 343.
3. Becker, *Denial,* ix.
4. Kinsley, "Death," 6.
5. Frankel, "News," 28.
6. Bittner, "Breathing," 16.
7. Fischer, *Medicine,* 206.
8. Gibbe, "In Utero Deaths," 54.
9. Diamond, "Celebrity AIDS," 16.
10. Ibid., 20.

Bibliography

Alali, A. Odasuo. "Management of Death and Grief in Obituary and In Memoriam Pages of Nigerian Newspapers." *Psychological Reports* 73, no. 3 (December 1993): 835–42.

Alpern, Sara, and Dale Baum. "Female Ballots: The Impact of the Nineteenth Amendment." *Journal of Interdisciplinary History* 16 (summer 1985): 43–69.

Amato, Joseph A. "Death and the Stories We Don't Have." *Monist* 76, no. 2 (April 1993): 252–69.

Ames, William E. *A History of the* National Intelligencer. Chapel Hill: University of North Carolina Press, 1972.

Aristotle. *The Nicomachean Ethics*. Trans. J. E. C. Welldon. Buffalo, N.Y.: Prometheus Books, 1987.

Barnard, Sylvia M. *To Prove I'm Not Forgot: Living and Dying in a Victorian City*. New York: Manchester University Press, 1990.

Beasley, Maurine H. "The Emergence of Modern Media." In *The Media in America: A History*, 3d ed., ed. William David Sloan and James D. Startt, 343–64. Northport, Ala.: Vision Press, 1996.

Becker, Ernest. *The Denial of Death*. New York: Free Press, 1973.

Bittner, Heidi. "Breathing Some Life into Routine Obits." *American Journalism Review* 16, no. 6 (July–August 1994): 16–17.

Bodnar, John. "Public Memory in an American City: Commemoration in Cleveland." In *Commemorations: The Politics of National Identity*, ed. John R. Gillis, 74–89. Princeton: Princeton University Press, 1994.

———. *Remaking America: Public Memory, Commemoration, and Patriotism in the Twentieth Century*. Princeton: Princeton University Press, 1992.

Boorstin, Daniel. *The Image: A Guide to Pseudo-Events in America*. New York: Atheneum, 1973.

Butler, Thomas, ed. *Memory: History, Culture, and the Mind*. Oxford: Basil Blackwell, 1989.

Bynum, W. F. *Science and the Practice of Medicine in the Nineteenth Century*. Cambridge: Cambridge University Press, 1994.

Chester, Edward W. "Lyndon Baines Johnson, an American 'King Lear': A Critical Evaluation of His Newspaper Obituaries." *Presidential Studies Quarterly* 21, no. 2 (spring 1991): 319–31.

Cohen, Akiba A., and Gadi Wolfsfeld, eds. *Framing the Intifada: People and the Media*. Norwood, N.J.: Ablex Publishers, 1993.

Connerton, Paul. *How Societies Remember*. New York: Cambridge University Press, 1989.

Cunningham, Noble E. *Popular Images of the Presidency from Washington to Lincoln*. Columbia: University of Missouri Press, 1991.

Curl, James Steven. *The Victorian Celebration of Death*. Detroit: Partridge Press, 1972.

Dabney, Thomas Ewing. *One Hundred Great Years: The Story of the Times-Picayune from Its Founding to 1940*. Baton Rouge: Louisiana State University Press, 1944.

Davidson, Cathy N. *Revolution and the Word: The Rise of the Novel in America*. New York: Oxford University Press, 1986.

Diamond, Edwin. "Celebrity AIDS." *New York Magazine*, 2 March 1987, 16–20.

Drake, Laura E., and William A. Donohue. "Communicative Framing Theory in Conflict Resolution." *Communication Research* 23, no. 3 (June 1996): 297–322.

Dublin, Thomas. *Women at Work*. New York: Columbia University Press, 1979.

Duffy, John. *Sword of Pestilence: The New Orleans Yellow Fever Epidemic of 1853*. Baton Rouge: Louisiana State University Press, 1966.

Elazar, Daniel. *Building toward Civil War: Generational Rhythms in American Politics*. Lanham, Md.: Madison Books, 1992.

Emery, Michael, and Edwin Emery. *The Press and America: An Interpretive*

History of the Mass Media. 6th ed. Englewood Cliffs, N.J.: Prentice-Hall, 1988.

Endres, Fredric F. "Frontier Obituaries as Cultural Reflectors: Toward 'Operationalizing' Carey's Thesis." *Journalism History* 11, nos. 3–4 (autumn–winter 1984): 54–60.

Entman, Robert M. "Framing: Toward Clarification of a Fractured Paradigm." *Journal of Communication* 43, no. 4 (1993): 51–58.

———. "Framing U.S. Coverage of International News." *Journal of Communication* 41, no. 4 (1991): 6–28.

Farrell, James J. *Inventing the American Way of Death, 1830–1920*. Philadelphia: Temple University Press, 1980.

Fischer, Heinz-Dietrich. *Medicine, Media, and Morality: Pulitzer Prize–Winning Writings on Health-Related Topics*. Malabar, Fla.: Krieger Publishing, 1992.

Foucault, Michel. *Discipline and Punish: The Birth of the Prison*. Trans. Alan Sheridan. New York: Vintage Books, 1979.

———. "Madness, the Absence of Work." Trans. Peter Stastny and Denis Sengel. *Critical Inquiry* 21 (winter 1995): 291–98.

———. *Power/Knowledge: Selected Interviews and Other Writings, 1972–1977*. Ed. and trans. Colin Gordon. New York: Pantheon Books, 1980.

Frankel, Max. "News of Lifetime." *New York Times Magazine*, 11 June 1995, 28.

French, Sean. "Death May Be Sting-Free, but Epitaphs and Obits Are Another Matter." *New Statesman and Society*, 9 September 1994, 33–34.

Gibbe, Dorothy. "In Utero Deaths: Should Newspapers Publish Obits?" *Editor and Publisher*, 22 April 1995, 54.

Gillis, John R., ed. *Commemorations: The Politics of National Identity*. Princeton: Princeton University Press, 1994.

Gitlin, Todd. *The Whole World Is Watching: Mass Media in the Making and Unmaking of the New Left*. Berkeley: University of California Press, 1980.

Glazer, Lee, and Susan Key. "Carry Me Back: Nostalgia for the Old South in Nineteenth-Century Popular Culture." *Journal of American Studies* 30, no. 1 (1996): 1–24.

Goffman, Erving. *Frame Analysis: An Essay on the Organization of Experience*. New York: Harper and Row, 1974.

Halbwachs, Maurice. *On Collective Memory*. Ed., trans., and intro. Lewis A. Coser. Chicago: University of Chicago Press, 1992.

Hareven, Tamara K. "The Search for Generational Memory: Tribal Rites in Industrial Society." *Daedalus* 106, no. 4 (fall 1978): 137–49.

Hartman, Geoffrey H. "Public Memory and Modern Experience." *Yale Journal of Criticism* 6, no. 2 (1993): 239–47.

Hartshorne, Thomas L., ed. *The Distorted Image: Changing Conceptions of the American Character since Turner*. Westport, Conn.: Greenwood Press, 1968.

Hartle, Ann. *Death and the Disinterested Spectator: An Inquiry into the Nature of Philosophy*. Albany: State University of New York Press, 1986.

Hollinger, Paul C. *Violent Deaths in the United States*. New York: Guilford Press, 1987.

Huyssen, Andreas. *Twilight Memories: Marking Time in a Culture of Amnesia*. New York: Routledge, 1995.

Iyengar, Shanto. *Is Anyone Responsible? How Television Frames Political Issues*. Chicago: University of Chicago Press, 1991.

Kammen, Michael. *Mystic Chords of Memory: The Transformation of Tradition in American Culture*. New York: Alfred A. Knopf, 1991.

Kastenbaum, Robert, Sara Peyton, and Beatrice Kastenbaum. "Sex Discrimination after Death." *Omega* 7, no. 4 (1976–77): 351–59.

Katzenstein, Mary Fainsod. "Constitutional Politics and the Feminist Movement." In *Voting and the Spirit of American Democracy: Essays on the History of Voting and Voting Rights in America*, ed. Donald W. Rogers, 83–96. Chicago: University of Chicago Press, 1992.

Kinsley, Michael. "Death Warmed Over." *New Republic*, 21 December 1992, 6.

Laderman, Gary. *The Sacred Remains: American Attitudes toward Death, 1799–1883*. New Haven: Yale University Press, 1996.

Lamb, Andrew W. "Freedom, the Self, and Ethical Practice According to Michel Foucault." *International Philosophical Quarterly* 35, no. 4 (December 1995): 449–67.

Lane, Roger. *Violent Death in the City*. Cambridge: Harvard University Press, 1979.

Lears, T. J. Jackson. *No Place of Grace: Antimodernism and the Transformation of American Culture, 1880–1920*. Chicago: University of Chicago Press, 1981.

Lemons, J. Stanley. *The Woman Citizen: Social Feminism in the 1920s*. Urbana: University of Illinois Press, 1973.

Lowenthal, David. "The Timeless Past: Some Anglo-American Historical Preconceptions." *Journal of American History* 75, no. 4 (March 1989): 1263–80.

Luxon, Norval Neal. Niles' Weekly Register: *News Magazine of the Nineteenth Century*. Baton Rouge: Louisiana State University Press, 1947.

MacDougall, Curtis D. *A College Course in Reporting for Beginners*. New York: Macmillan, 1932.

Maulsby, William S. *Getting the News*. New York: Harcourt, Brace, 1925.

"Michael Quinn Writes Capsule Obituaries for *Time*'s Milestones Section." *Time*, 2 October 1995, 4.

Morone, James A. "The Struggle for American Culture." *PS: Political Science and Politics* 20, no. 3 (September 1996): 424–31.

Mott, Frank Luther. *American Journalism: A History of Newspapers in the United States through 250 Years, 1690 to 1940*. New York: Macmillan, 1945.

———. *A History of American Magazines, 1741–1850*. New York: D. Appleton, 1930.

Noiriel, Gerald. "Foucault and History: The Lessons of a Disillusion." *Journal of Modern History* 66 (September 1994): 547–68.

Norris, Pippa, ed. *Women, Media, and Politics*. New York: Oxford University Press, 1997.

Pan, Zhongdang, and Gerald M. Kosicki. "Framing Analysis: An Approach to News Discourse." *Political Communication* 10 (January–March 1993): 55–76.

Pettegrew, John. "'The Soldier's Faith': Turn-of-the-Century Memory of the Civil War and the Emergence of Modern American Nationalism." *Journal of Contemporary History* 31 (1996): 49–73.

Porter, Philip W., and Norval Neil Luxon. *The Reporter and the News*. New York: D. Appleton- Century, 1935.

Potter, David M. *People of Plenty: Economic Abundance and the American Character*. Chicago: University of Chicago Press, 1954.

Remini, Robert V. *Andrew Jackson and the Course of American Democracy, 1833–1845*. Vol. 3. New York: Harper and Row, 1984.

———. *The Election of Andrew Jackson*. Philadelphia: J. B. Lippincott, 1963.

Rogers, Donald W., ed. *Voting and the Spirit of American Democracy: Essays on the History of Voting and Voting Rights in America*. Chicago: University of Chicago Press, 1992.

Roniger, Luis. "From Eulogy to Announcement: Death Notices in the Jewish Press since the Late Eighteenth Century." *Omega* 25, no. 2 (1992): 133–68.

Rose, Anne C. *Victorian America and the Civil War*. New York: Cambridge University Press, 1992.

Ross, Charles G. *The Writing of News*. New York: Henry Holt, 1911.

Ryan, Mary P. *The Cradle of the Middle Class: The Family in Oneida County, New York, 1790–1865*. New York: Cambridge University Press, 1981.

Schlozman, Kay Lehman, Nancy Burns, Sidney Verba, and Jesse Donahue.

"Gender and Citizen Participation: Is There a Different Voice?" *American Journal of Political Science* 39, no. 2 (May 1995): 267–93.

Schudson, Michael. *The Power of News.* Cambridge: Harvard University Press, 1995.

———. *Watergate in American Memory: How We Remember, Forget, and Reconstruct the Past.* New York: HarperCollins, 1992.

Schwartz, Barry. "Social Change and Collective Memory: The Democratization of George Washington." *American Sociological Review* 56 (April 1991): 221–36.

———. "The Social Context of Commemoration: A Study in Collective Memory." *Social Forces* 6, no. 2 (December 1982): 374–402.

Sloan, William David, and James D. Startt, eds. *The Media in America: A History.* 3d ed. Northport, Ala.: Vision Press, 1996.

Sloane, David Charles. *The Last Great Necessity: Cemeteries in American History.* 1991. Reprint, Baltimore: Johns Hopkins University Press, 1995.

Stevenson, Louise L. *The Victorian Homefront: American Thought and Culture,* 1860–1880. New York: Twayne Publishers, 1991.

Susman, Warren I. *Culture as History: The Transformation of American Society in the Twentieth Century.* New York: Pantheon Books, 1984.

Thelen, David. "Memory and American History." *Journal of American History* 75, no. 4 (March 1989): 1117–29.

Tocqueville, Alexis de. *Democracy in America.* Vol. 2, ed. Phillips Bradeley. New York: Vintage Books, 1945.

Tuchman, Gaye. *Making News: A Study in the Construction of Reality.* New York: Free Press, 1978.

Ward, John William. *Andrew Jackson: Symbol for an Age.* New York: Oxford University Press, 1962.

Warner, W. Lloyd. *The Living and the Dead: A Study of the Symbolic Life of Americans.* New Haven: Yale University Press, 1959.

Watson, Harry L. "In Retrospect: The Venturous Conservative Reconsidered: Social History and Political Culture in the Market Revolution." *Reviews in American History* 22, no. 4 (December 1994): 732–40.

Webster, Noah. *A Compendious Dictionary of the English Language.* 1806. Reprint, New York: Bounty Books, 1970.

Webster, William. *High School Pronouncing Dictionary of the English Language.* New York: Mason Brothers, 1856.

Welter, Rush. *The Mind of America,* 1820–1860. New York: Columbia University Press, 1975.

Whaley, Joachim. *Mirrors of Mortality: Studies in the Social History of Death.* New York: St. Martin's Press, 1981.

Wheeler, Michael. *Heaven, Hell, and the Victorians.* Cambridge: Cambridge University Press, 1994.

Wilson, Timothy H. "Foucault, Genealogy, History." *Philosophy Today*, summer 1995, 157–70.

Index